Modern Poetry in T
Series Three, Numl

GW00383678

Parnassus

Edited by David and Helen Constantine

MODERN POETRY IN TRANSLATION

Modern Poetry in Translation
Series Three, No. 17
© Modern Poetry in Translation 2012 and contributors
ISBN 978-0-9559064-9-7

Printed and bound in Great Britain by Charlesworth Press, Wakefield

Submissions should be sent in hard copy, with return postage, to David
and Helen Constantine, *Modern Poetry in Translation*, The Queen's College,
Oxford, OX1 4AW. Unless agreed in advance, submissions by email will
not be accepted. Only very exceptionally will we consider work that has
already been published elsewhere. Translators are themselves responsible
for obtaining any necessary permissions, and should be aware that work
published in *MPT* may also appear on our website and as an e-book, and
will be accessible to readers who have subscribed to the digital version of
the magazine.

Subscription Rates: (including postage)

	UK	Overseas
Single Issue	£9.95	£12.50 / US$ 21
One year subscription (2 issues, surface mail)	£19.90	£25.00 / US$ 42
Two year subscription (4 issues, surface mail)	£36.00	£46.00 / US$ 77

To subscribe please use the subscription form at the back of the magazine.
Discounts available.

To pay by credit card please visit www.mptmagazine.com

Modern Poetry in Translation is represented in the UK by
Central Books, 99 Wallis Road, London, E9 5LN

For orders: tel +44 (0) 845 458 9911 Fax +44 (0) 845 458 9912
or visit www.mptmagazine.com

Modern Poetry in Translation Limited. A Company Limited by Guarantee.
Registered in England and Wales, Number 5881603.
UK Registered Charity Number 1118223.

Contents

POETRY PARNASSUS

Reviews

Editorial

The games at Olympia, together with those at Nemea, Delphi and Corinth, were occasions on which the Greeks affirmed their sense of being Greek. There was no Greek nation, but there were many tribes, local dynasties, city states, confederations; and coming together for the games or for the great religious festivals at Eleusis, on the island of Delos and elsewhere, they knew what they had in common, as Greeks. Self-identity is always a matter not just of what you are but also of what you are not; and the Greeks felt themselves to be Greek by virtue of not being barbarians, the obvious marker of barbarians being that they did not speak Greek but made brutish and unintelligible sounds instead. A 'barbarism' is a linguistic usage not in accordance with the classical language, not the Queen's English.

When Baron Pierre de Coubertin revived the Olympic Games in 1896 (after visiting the Olympians in Much Wenlock, see Anna Selby's essay in this issue), 14 nations and 241 athletes competed in 43 events. He started an idea of world-wide inclusivity and in that spirit, with many lapses, travesties and gross aberrations, so the Games, and the Paralympics joining them, have developed to what they are now, 204 nations, more than 14000 men and women competing. So the identity of the modern Games, ideally, is inclusive, not exclusive: an extraordinary variety of participants, all to be welcomed and respected, coming together in one place in voluntary and peaceful (not belligerent, not merciless, not lethal) competition.

We were very pleased and proud at *MPT* when we were invited to participate in the South Bank's 'Poetry Parnassus', in fact to be the magazine in which at least a few of the hundreds of arriving poets and translators would find lodgings. It is the happiest match: our magazine with that assembly. Each issue under our editorship has been an anthology of many voices, a medley, an ensemble, and intrinsically an act of faith in human coexistence in variety. And more and more lately, and with a further extension in this present issue, *MPT*, edited in Oxford, has been connected to the world wide web. One book, 200 pages between two covers, reaching into and being reached by the whole world. The South Bank at the end of June will be a locus like a physical book, more various still, more bursting out of the covers – all those poets and translators – translators who *are* poets – assembling in one place on the riverbank of a great city that speaks five hundred languages in its homes.

The day after the 2012 Olympic Games were awarded to London, 52 people were murdered in the city by four Britons. Glance at the obituaries of those dead Londoners, dead visitors and guests in London, the mix is the very hallmark of what the city is and represents, all kinds of people, all manner of achievements and aspirations, creeds, origins, ancestries. When four implacably hating young men put bombs on a London bus and the London tube the blast travelled far beyond the city and the British Isles, it struck at families in Poland, Kenya, Afghanistan, Sri Lanka, Turkey, Vietnam, Ghana, Nigeria, Mauritius and many other countries too. We are all connected.

The Ancient Greeks were a notably quarrelsome and belligerent people. Sharing a culture, speaking varieties of the same language, certain they were not barbarians, frequently they embroiled themselves in internecine strife. The Olympic Games, held in Elis, were in essence a religious festival because in that place Zeus had a great sanctuary and people came to worship there. So for the duration of the Games, five days, and for some time either side of that period, a cessation of hostilities was imposed on all the competing parties, many of whom would inevitably be at war with one another. Indeed Elis, even when no Games were in progress, became a land which armies en route to fight elsewhere were only allowed to pass through if they agreed to give up their weapons on entering and get them back on leaving. Many competitors will arrive in London this summer from homelands at war internally and abroad. And the cost of 'peace' (security) in the host city has risen to more than £1bn. There will be 7500 troops (and 23,700 'security personnel') on duty at the venues and a battleship on the Thames. This is to secure a space in which competitors can compete in peace.

A few years ago the fires wasting large areas of Greece came very close to the site at Olympia. And a month ago two armed and masked men held up the only guard on duty and stole seventy-seven exhibits from the museum, among them a bronze statuette of a victorious athlete and a bronze charioteer in Geometric style. Much is under threat, much feels to be slip-sliding away. This magazine, the South Bank, the many venues, may they be safe places for some things of value.

Helen and David Constantine
March 2012

The Next Issue of *MPT*

The next issue of *Modern Poetry in Translation* (Third Series, Number 18, Autumn 2012) will be called 'Transitions'.

The present issue, 'Parnassus', is the last under our sole editorship. The next issue, 'Transitions', will be jointly edited by us and whoever succeeds us. So in that obvious sense the autumn issue will be transitional. But we are looking for contributions which will address the whole concept of transition in as many ways as possible. First, perhaps, as it might be applied to the theory and practice of translation itself, the going across from one language and from one text to another, from native to foreign, to and fro. Some translators actually strive to make their translation *a thing in transition*, partaking of both worlds and hovering between the foreign and the native. Many feel translations to be always 'transitional', since most (unlike the texts being translated) date quickly, and have to be done again for new readers coming along in successive generations. More widely: if, as Heraclitus thought, 'eveything moves and flows', no writing true to life can desire fixity, let alone achieve it; and some poets have made a virtue of the fact that everything is in flux. We invite translated poems, short essays, anecdotes, that will address the idea of transition. Perhaps the translations themselves will be the demonstration, the process. This volume will celebrate movement, flux, change, the eternal (and hopeful) possibility of moving on out of forms and ways of thinking that have lost their liberating and enlivening force, and into new ones, that will work. By its very diversity *MPT* always has acted against set minds. We want 'Transitions' to be proof and promise that we always shall.

Submissions should be sent by 15 August 2012, please, in hard copy, with return postage, to The Editors, *Modern Poetry in Translation*, The Queen's College, Oxford, OX1 4AW. Unless agreed in advance, submissions by email will not be accepted. Only very exceptionally will we consider work that has already been published elsewhere. Translators are themselves responsible for obtaining and, if required, paying for any necessary permissions. Contributors should be aware that work published in *MPT* may also appear on our website and as an ebook, and will be accessible to readers who have subscribed to the digital version of the magazine. Permissions should cover this.

Helen and David Constantine
March 2012

Pindar
Victory Odes
Translated from the Ancient Greek by
Cameron Hawke Smith

Pindar's Odes were a celebration of life as expressed in what was for the Greeks its supreme form: excellence in individual competitive games. He used all the resources available to him to achieve this celebration: intricate patterns of dance and music as well as patterns of words. We have to imagine the chorus creating a series of complex visual patterns on the floor, as they turned to face different sections of the audience in the circular theatre. Within the word patterns he weaves stories or fragments of stories of the gods, who created the games and whose presence is everywhere felt in the landscape and family histories of the athletes. They are the eternal spectators.

With so much richness it is no wonder Pindar has proved hard to translate. We have to select some aspect of the poetry. My versions place all the emphasis on the imagery of the poems, mainly visual but also, I believe, kinetic. I try to catch a little of the dance movement in the flow of the words on the page. The English language with its strength in monosyllables and simple rhythms is entirely unlike ancient Greek with its polysyllables, its quantitative metres and its pitch accent. But we share images and resources of metaphor, though sometimes we must unpick

these from the deep etymological roots of our common linguistic
heritage.

From Olympian I

For Hieron of Syracuse,
winner in the horse-race, 476 BCE

Water is best of all things
and what rich man's hoard
is more than small change when set
against the blazing splendour
of gold at night?

Or which star
old heart can compete
with the sun for warmth?
And where are the contenders
amongst games with those of Olympia?

So poets stitch songs to its fabled cloak
celebrating Zeus
at the opulent hearth of Hieron
whose kingdom is Sicily
island of sheepgrass –
a just man with a shepherd's baton

Famed connoisseur
his fingers gather
the choicest arts of the Muses
as the softest down of a fleece
We poets make sport
around a friendly table

So take up the lyre
if you felt a sharp frisson
of joy as without a spur
the horse Pherénikos outpaced all

Victorious

bringing home the prize for his master
soldier king and horseman
a blazing star in this great band
of competing athletes

The good things of daily life
that come to all are best

but winners of Olympic glory
will breathe a honeyed air
for all their days
and I will walk among them
with a torch of praise

from Olympian XIV

For Asopikhos of Orkhomenos
winner in the foot-race, 488 BCE

queens of song
queens of the rich
horse-grazings of Orkhómenos
three lady graces hear my prayer

potni' Aglaía
      Euphrosúna
            Thalía

lady fame
lady wit
lady body-beautiful
lovers of the dance
heaven's impresarios

never was man wise
or handsome or famous
nor could even the gods
lay out a feast or a dance floor
without your guidance

help me compose
in celebration of Asópikhos
a lightfoot dance
in the Lydian mode

and Ekho
go to the dark walls
of Persephóna's
house of the dead
and bear the news to his father

tell Kleódamos how victory
in the famous valleys of Pisa
has placed wings
on the young man's
mane of hair

from Pythian XII

For Midas of Akragas, winner in piping 490 BCE

fair city of Akragas
take this garland
and with it take famous Midas
and his winning art of music

three snakehead sister monsters
stood against Perseus
the golden youth

a slash of his sword
struck dead a third part of them
and out of the mouthings of grief

death's hollow catcall

Athana fingered a tune
the polycephalic tune that woos
multitudes to the games

a breathing through delicate bronze
or through reeds
from the beds of Kaphisos
the Graces' dancing place

from Olympian III

For Theron of Akragas, winner in the chariot-race

Herakles in pursuit of the doe
with the golden antler
came to the land
beyond the north wind's home

and wondered
at the forest of dark green
(for which there is no word in Greek)
and the round eye of the moon
gazed at him

a sweet urge came upon him
to fetch that primal greenness
and make shade for the racetrack

where the garden
with the consecrated altars of Zeus
was naked of trees and exposed
to the sun's caustic rays

and now athletes
hot from the chase
and crowned
by the Arbiter of Games
carry that forest on their victors' heads

Pindar
Olympian XIV
For Asopichos of Orchomenos, winner in the foot-race
A version by David Constantine from Hölderlin's translation into German

In the summer of 1800 Hölderlin translated some 2000 lines of Pindar, cleaving very close to the Greek, word-for-word, indeed syllable-for-syllable where he could. Though the manuscript looks like fair copy, he seems never to have had any intention of publishing these translations. They were an exercise, a devoted labour, by which he came into the language he needed for his future work. The German of his translation, so ghosted by the Greek, foreshadows the language of his 'Pindaric' hymns a year later, a language uniquely his own. My version of 'Olympian XIV' does not keep so closely to Hölderlin's German as he did to Pindar's Greek. German is an inflecting language, like Greek; it can indicate grammatical relations between words quite far apart, much better than English can. So Hölderlin's Pindar-German, difficult enough to follow without the Greek, would have been almost unintelligible had I proceeded strictly in his fashion.

A few notes.

This River Cephissus (another flowed near Athens, past Plato's Academy) rises on Mount Parnassus from a spring said to roar at noon like a bull, and empties into Lake Copais, in Boeotia, at Orchomenos, a very ancient town. Pindar was from Boeotia.

The Charites, later known as the Graces, give and oversee much that makes life enjoyable. The Cephissus was sacred to them.

Pisa, in Elis, was close to where the Games were held.

Asopichus' father, Cleodemus, is dead. Pindar sends Echo into Hades, to tell him the good news.

Olympian XIV

O sovereign Charites, singers of the many songs,
In shining Orchomenos where
By the waters of Cephissus foals in their beauty
Come and go, you watchers over the long-
Since rooted house
Of Minyas, hear my prayer. With you
All that is sweet and cheerful
Ensues to us
Mortals if wise, if beautiful, if noble
Any is. For not even the gods
Can command the lands and the feasts
Except with the holy Charites who foster
All that is done in heaven and set their thrones
In the house of Pythian Apollo
Of the golden bow and tend the glory
Of boundless Olympian
Zeus.

Bright Aglaia, and you, the lover of songs
Euphrosyne, daughters of the strongest of all the gods
Listen now, watch with Thalia in whom
Song is the laughter of happiness
The dancers lightly accompanying a sweet good fortune
And hear this paean that I
Whose care is song
Bring in the Lydian mode
For Asopichus who has brought through you
At Olympia
Victory to the house of Minyas. Go now, Echo
To the black-walled house of Persephone
And bring to the father, to Cleodemus, this glorious news
And, seeing him, say his son
In the lap of famous Pisa
Has crowned his hair
With the wings of the sovereign contest.

Constantine Cavafy
Four poems
Translated from the Greek by Ian Parks

Constantine Cavafy died in Alexandria – the city in which he had spent most of his life – in 1933. Shortly before his death at the age of seventy he took Holy Communion at the Orthodox Church. His last act was to trace a circle on a piece of paper and then place a full-stop in its centre. It was a suitably enigmatic end to a life in which he wrote poems almost in secret, shunning publication and sharing them with a select circle of friends. His reputation as one of the finest Greek poets of the twentieth century came only after his death with the publication in 1935 of his first collection. W.H. Auden drew attention to Cavafy's 'unique tone of voice', claiming that it 'survives translation'. These versions form part of *The Cavafy Variations,* due for publication by Rack Press in 2013.

The God Abandons Anthony

It's midnight now. Outside you hear
the music and the voices as they fade –
the unseen dancers passing in the street,
the songs they sang diminishing.
It's not the time to have regrets,
to brood upon the glories of your past
or curse the good luck you once had
now that it's faltering, running low.
Those things were just illusions.
As if you were prepared to face the loss
draw courage to your heart and say farewell
to Alexandria as she slips away.
Don't claim it was some waking dream;
that what you saw and said were all unreal.
Don't shirk the pain that wells up in your soul.
You know there's nothing left to say.
As if you were prepared to face the loss
step out onto the balcony, look down,
and listen, stirred, to what you heard before;
not cheering crowds but the last sounds
of the city leaving, emptying.
Then smile with pleasure as you say farewell
to Alexandria as she slips away.

Unfaithfulness

Apollo, guest of honour at the lavish wedding feast
blessed Peleus and Thetis, wished them joy.
She would give birth to a beautiful son:
untouched by sickness, he'd live long.
Thetis was contented when she heard
the future set out for her newborn boy
by Apollo, shimmering god of prophecy.
Achilles grew to be a healthy child
and many times his mother would recall
his promise and his words of gold.
And then she heard the news:
her son, the great Achilles had been killed,
fighting for the Greeks outside the gates of Troy.
She tore the seams of her purple dress,
threw her rings and bracelets in the sea,
poured ashes on her head, cried to the sky.
Where was Apollo when this came to pass?
The messengers were speechless.
Apollo himself had gone down to Troy,
was there in person when they killed her son,
when they stuck him like a pig and bled him dry.

As Kleitos Lies Dying

Kleitos had it all: youth, an education,
enough Greek to impress.
All that counts for nothing now he's ill —
struck down by a disease
that cut through Alexandria like a scythe.

The fever hit him unawares,
still grieving for the actor friend he'd loved
who'd loved him back then took his love away.

His parents stand in silence
in the sick-room where he lies,
burned up and scarcely breathing on the bed.

And so the nurse who'd raised him as a child,
as fearful and as anxious as the rest
recalls the god she worshipped long ago
before the Christian household took her in
a servant girl who, like them, turned to Christ.

All she can remember are a few disjointed prayers.
She whispers them intently,
brings bowls of honey, wine and bread,
and places them before the flickering shrine:
an offering to the much-neglected god.
She prays on deluded. She doesn't realise
that the idol is impervious;
it doesn't hear or care
if a Christian like Kleitos lives or dies.

The Deadline

Nero shrugged his shoulders when he heard
the future that Apollo prophesied:
Beware the age of seventy-three.
The oracle at Delphi never lied;
he took her at her word.
Untroubled, he slept on secure.

At thirty he could dedicate his life
to pleasure pure and simple, unperturbed,
the deadline more than forty years away.

Jaded, he limps back to Rome
hung-over from his trip to Greece,
transformed, translated by excess:
the actors, races, stadiums, flowing wine,
Achaean cities sloping to the shore
with naked bodies lolling on the beach,
stars reflected in the purple sea...

So Nero dreams. And meanwhile
on the arid flats of Spain
Galba drills his legions secretly.
Galba, a sprightly seventy-three.

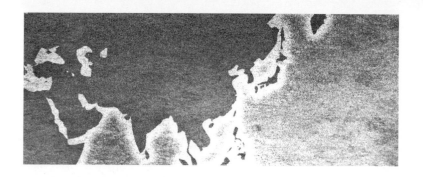

Li Bai (701–762 A.D.)
Three poems
Translated by Julian Farmer

Li Bai, who was for a long time in the West known as Li Po, is China's most celebrated ancient poet. He is one of the poets of the Tang Dynasty, whose canon is the most frequently read and translated of all periods of Chinese poetry. His style is more direct and heartrending than, say, the tranquillity of Wang Wei, and he sometimes employs more modern rhyming schemes, but he is also thought to embody a traditional approach, especially in his imitation of folk songs.

Night thoughts

In front of my bed, there is bright moonlight,
which makes me wonder if there's frost on the floor.
I raise my head to look at the bright moon.
I droop my head, and think of my home town . . .

Spring thoughts

The grasses of Yan are like emerald silk.
In Qin, the mulberries droop green branches.
When the gentleman longs for day to return,
it's his mistress's time for heartbreak.
The spring breezes do not know themselves...
What came in, and caught the curtain of my bed?

Song from Wu Region
In the style of Lady Ziye

In Chang'an, there's a slip of moon,
and the sound of ten thousand households, beating clothes.
The autumn wind blows, ceaselessly,
but my affections always turn towards Yu Pass.
When will the enemy be put down and imprisoned,
and my good man finish his long expedition?

Michael Mackmin
'My Sweet Redhead'
An imitation of Guillaume Apollinaire's
'La Jolie Rousse'

So, here I stand, a man of sense and feeling
knowledgeable about life and knowing
as much about death as any living
man can know. Yes, I've tried love,
its famous agonies and ecstasies:
I'm quite good at ideas – so some say –
fluent in several languages,
have knocked about the world a bit,
I've seen war as a gunner (culpable
of dishing out 'friendly' fire) and
as a foot soldier (the ones that get it
from both sides); I had a head wound –
got trepanned while under the ether –
and the war, grisly farce, slaughtered my best friends.

Let's go, you and me, put aside the war,
consider, as students of history, people
pretty well up in today's thinking,
this terminal quarrel
tradition v creativity
order v experiment.

You who speak for God
whose mouths are godlike
who speak for unalterable
order, please, can we beg
a little leeway? When
stood up against your saints,
your imams, your perfect
poets with their exact
hexameters, all that
manifestation of order's
perfection: forgive us
our louche insistence
on adventure, on difference.

We Are Not Your Enemies
We can see that there are vast
blanks on the mind's maps, Terrae
Incognitae, jungles of desire, new
fires, colours never before seen
a million inexplicable fantasies
to nail into the human skull.

Above all else there is the necessary
exploration of kindness, that republic
of enormous gentle silences
Above all we are stuck here
fighting on the frontiers of tomorrow,
of infinity, wrestling with time
bending it, re-shaping it
Can you not pity us, can you not
wring a little compassion out of
your closed and dogmatic hearts?

Look, another violent summer comes raging in
my young years are dead as spring in the trenches
O sun, sun, Reason is going down in flames
but I'm still here waiting. Her
passionate pilgrim watching
as she changes shape
becomes noble and gentle, enchants me,
and as I fall for her she pulls at me
a magnet for the bullet in my heart.

Whoever your angel is, mine
is that sweet red-haired woman
with that red-gold hair
flickering like lightning
on, on, on, or flames
spreading up, peacock tails
of heat, the flare-up
of old roses just as they
blow and fade.

Umberto Saba
Three football poems
Versions from the Italian by Martin Bennett

Born when Trieste was still part of the Austro-Hungarian
Empire and had regular rail links with Vienna, Umberto Poli
(1883–1957) changed his name to Saba, Hebrew for bread, with
the publication of his first book of poems. This was partly in
honour of his Jewish mother whom Saba's father, Edoardo Poli,
had effectively abandoned when she was pregnant. Taking his
cue from Petrarch and Heine, Saba's first and the subsequent
volumes form part of what he liked to think of as a complete
work entitled 'Canzoniere', tracing the development of his life
as in a novel. Self-analysis (an early sonnet sequence dissects his
relationship – or lack of it – with his absent father) and often
painful biography are counterbalanced by a closeness to the
community, or more particularly 'Triestinità' as one critic has
called it. (Both aspects are apparent in the football poems here.)
The Vienna connection is often as important as the Italian one:
In 1929 Saba underwent psychoanalysis under Edoardo Weiss, a
student of Freud. The autobiographical element of Saba's verse
plus his sharp-eyed concern for the everyday tended to set him
apart from other Italian poets – first from D'Annunzio whom
Saba took issue with for his 'disonestà', then from the avantgarde
and later the Hermetic movement of the 1930s. Yet, in an

exemplary instance of solidarity among poets, it was Ungaretti in Rome and then Montale in Florence who helped shelter Saba from Nazi persecution when he had to flee Trieste in 1943. His last volume – *Six poems of old age* – brought, albeit posthumously, his 'Canzoniere' (1961) to completion.

Three football poems

Umberto Saba was not only a poet. He was also, as evidenced by his 'Five poems on the game of football', a keen supporter of 'il rosso alabardi' (halberds, on the team's badge.) In these poems the two passions combine, Trieste's 'Reds' co-opted by the poet as embodying 'that epic of everyday' which characterizes the rest of his verse. 'The game of football becomes the game of life', in the words of another critic. To quote Saba himself, 'For the poet the players are true heroes with a resemblance to the *kalos kai agathos* of Homeric myth.' In the translator this kicks off an unlikely but delightful scenario: One fine day, to counter the ever-growing commercialization of sport, teams could display not money-grubbing company logos, but the names of poets and even, jersey space allowing, their verses. (Writers of haikus and epigrams would be at an advantage in this regard.)

'Passione' in Italy is a word frequently applied to sports in contradistinction to the Anglo-Saxon 'stiff upper lip', or what remains of it: 'If you can meet with Triumph and Disaster and treat those two impostors just the same, . . . you'll be a Man, my son.' In the three poems here, the reaction to those 'two imposters' is anything but Kiplingesque. An Anglo-Saxon midfield equivalent of Saba's goalie, Paul Gascoigne in the 1990 World Cup Finals wept openly into his shirt after England were eliminated, only for him to be promptly signed up by Lazio. For Italians, Gascoigne (aka Gazzicoigne), though English, had demonstrated the necessary 'passione' of 'un vero campione'. (The same could also be applied to volleyball, basketball, water polo, fencing, etc.)

Win or lose, as in opera, it is the emotion that counts. Or, again to quote Saba: 'What is there to say when a small town team scores a goal against a team in the league (whose superiority is often money-based), so resurrecting in the dewy eyes of its local supporters the miracle of David defeating over again Goliath.'

Commenting on the final poem, the poet's own favourite, Saba writes:

'Tredicesima partita' was not played in Trieste. Nor was the local team – 'rossi alabardati' – or the Reds – taking part. The poet found himself together with his daughter in Padua. The match was an end of season play-off between Padua and another team whose name I've forgotten. For Padua, losing would have meant demotion to the second division. One can imagine the state of mind of the few Paduans present; few, because the match was being played on a weekday. Padua were up against a much stronger team; worse still they were not in form. Then one of their players, at the last minute, fell ill; he was replaced by a player who was not only old but overweight. Not having played for quite some time, it seemed he would not be able to complete the match, only for him to score the winning goal. The crowd, needless to say, went mad.

As regards rhyme, Saba is, when necessary, a past master, slotting them in with the precision of a topnotch striker, even when not expected. 'Quality written all over them', to adopt a phrase. To conserve as far as possible the effect in English, I admit, especially in 'Goal', to having resorted to adding here and there a word not in the original. For example, in the case of 'pressing' to translate 'si accalca (in l. 5 of 'Three Moments'), the term is an 'anglicismo' used by Italian football commentators week in week out, along with 'stopper', 'assist', 'mister', 'bomber', etc. In fact a whole essay could be devoted to Italo-English borrowings in football alone. Also the term helps project that match back in the thirties into the age of satellite tv; the same can be said for 'Heaven turns camera' to render 'è dato, sotto cielo, di vedere' in 'Goal'.

'Traduttore, traditore', one might argue, to repeat an Italian proverb, one of those mysterious semantic/phonetic coincidences like English's womb/ tomb. Conversely, though, it is rhyme which helps make a poem a poem as opposed to just another wad of prose. In short the task of the translator is never an easy one. Rhyme or no rhyme, it is a case of 'damned if you do, damned if you don't.'

To further excuse the odd lexical inaccuracy, one could also cite the rather grander examples of Pound, Robert Lowell and Christopher Logue's dazzlingly cross-cultural *Iliad*. All tread a thin but fascinating line between translation and improvisation – or 'making it new'; the letter of the original gets sometimes sidestepped so as to better maintain its spirit.

From 'Five poems on the game of football'

Late goal

Spread-eagled across his goal line
keeper bites mud and quicklime
to parry the bitterness of light.
Fullback kneels, levers him upright
now with words, and then with hands
only to notice his eyes are wet.

Crowd's fit to bust the terraces –
a drunken oneness – the scorer theirs,
team mates flung about his neck.
To all those gnawed by love and hate
this is about as good as it gets,
moments where heaven turns camera.

His own goal intact, other keeper
stays put. Or in body at least.
His soul, joyfully joining the rest,
performs an empathic somersault,
blows kisses north, south, east, west.
At this party – he says – count me in.

Three moments

Having run out onto the pitch, salute
first the stands. Next,
for what comes next,
you must turn away, up against
something darker, its pressing
beyond words, which has no name.

Goalie strides to-and-fro, the same
as a sentry. Danger till now
keeps its distance, though,
if in a cloud it nears, low
crouches a wild young beast
and keeps look out.

Celebration is in the air, each street.
If over so little, so what?
No striker has hit the back of the net,
cheers like rockets crisscrossed heaven:
Glory boys, our own eleven –
love a river that bedecks Trieste.

Last game

On the terraces a meagre gaggle
was generating its own heating.
And when –
less ray than flash – behind a house
the sun quenched its glare, the pitch
paved the way for nightfall.
The red jerseys ran back and forth,
so did the whites, both weirdly lit up
as by a rainbow. Then wind
deflected the ball: Luck
had put back on her blindfold.
What pleasure –
we few, we happy few
shivering united,
like the last of mankind on a mountaintop,
watching the final Final.

Mary-Ann Constantine
'Canu Penillion': singing stanzas to the harp in Wales

As Thomas Pennant made his way through the mountains of Snowdonia, observing castles and cairns, fine views and interesting plants, he was also keen to inform his readers of his country's more picturesque customs:

> Some vein of the antient minstrelsie is still to be met with in these mountainous countries. Numbers of persons, of both sexes, assemble, and sit around the harp, singing alternately *pennylls*, or stanzas of antient or modern poetry. The young people usually begin the night with dancing, and when they are tired, sit down, and assume this species of relaxation. Oftentimes, like the modern *Improvisatore* of *Italy*, they will sing extempore verses. A person conversant in this art, will produce a *pennyll* apposite to the last which was sung: the subjects produce a great deal of mirth; for they are sometimes jocular, at others satyrical, and many amorous. They will continue singing without intermission, and never repeat the same stanza; for that would occasion the loss of honor of being held first of the song . . .
>
> (*Tour in Wales*, 1781).

No one quite knows how much faith to put in these early accounts of the practice (even at the time some thought he was laying it on a bit thick: 'here we are to understand,' wrote one snooty reviewer, 'that every Welsh shepherd and plowman is an *improvisatore*'). But it is clear that some form of contrapuntal singing to the harp has been practised in Welsh for centuries, and that it has changed with time and musical fashions. Today *Canu Penillion* forms one of the competitions in the national Eisteddfod, where the trick is to sing in a particular way against the tune of the harp. Hundreds of single verse stanzas – the *penillion* – have been collected and recorded since Pennant's time. T. H. Parry-Williams's *Hen Benillion* (1940) has over 700 of them; Glyn Jones, *A People's Poetry* (1977) puts a selection into English verse.

They are lovely things, pared down and heart-catching like the landscapes they often evoke, and quite impossible to translate. But I have done some here, very simply:

Dacw'r llwyn o fedw nwyfus   See: a grove of restless birch
Dacw seren y tair ynys   See: the star of three isles
Dacw fab â'r olwg tirion   See: the lad with beauty in his face
Dacw toriad llawer calon   See: the breaker of many hearts

O f'anwylyd, cyfod frwynen   Oh beloved, take a reed
Ac ymafael yn ei deupen   And grasp it at both ends
Yn ei hanner tor hi'n union   Break it in half, exactly,
Fel y torraist ti fy nghalon   As you broke my heart

Mi eis i garu dros y mynydd   I went after love over the mountain
Yn fy sanau gwynion newyddion   In my finest white stockings
Wrth fynd trwy hen gorsydd   But going through the soaking bog
  gwlybion
Cefais bâr o sanau duon   They ended up filthy black

Pan fo gas gan hen gath lefrith
Pan fo gas gan g'lomen wenith
Pan fo gas gan alarch nofio
Dyna pryd y dof i'ch ceisio

When the old cat is sick of milk
When the dove is sick of wheat
When the swan is sick of swimming –
Then I'll come round your place
        courting

Maent yn dywedyd y ffordd yma
Nad oes dim mor oer â'r eira
Rhois ychydig yn fy mynwes
Clywn yr eira oer yn gynnes

Round here they will tell you
That nothing is so cold as snow:
I put a little of it on my breast
And the cold snow felt warm to me

Ar lan y mor heli ni thyfodd
    erioed
Na bedwen na gwernen na
    draenen ar droed
Nac un math o goedydd ond
    llwyni o frwyn;
Dan gysgod y rheini daw defaid
    ac wyn

By the salt salt sea there never grew

Birch or ash or even thorn

Nor any kind of tree, but acres of
    reeds
Under them shelter the lambs and
    sheep

Gwyn eu byd yr adar gwylltion
Hwy gânt fynd y ffordd a fynnon',
Rhai tua'r môr a rhai tua'r mynydd
A dŵad adref yn ddigerydd.

Blessed the small wild birds
Who can go wherever they like
Some to the sea, some to the hills
And home again, unpunished

Hawdd yw dwedyd 'dacw'r
    Wyddfa'
Nid eir trosti ond yn ara'

Easy to say: 'look there's Snowdon':

It's a slow enough business getting
    over.

Hawdd i'r iach, a fo'n ddiddolur

Easy for those who are well, in no
    pain,

Beri i'r afiach gymryd cysur

To urge the sick to take comfort

Gwynt ar fôr a haul ar fynydd
Cerrig llwydion yn lle coedydd
A gwylanod yn lle dynion
Och Dduw! Pa fodd na thorrai
    'nghalon?

Wind on the sea, sun on the mountain
Slate-grey stones in place of trees
And gulls instead of people
God! Why does my heart not break?

Deryn bach â'i bluen sidan
A'i big aur, a'i dafod arian:
Dacw'r tŷ a dacw'r sgubor

Dacw'r beudy a'r drws yn agor
Dacw'r dderwen fawr yn tyfu
A'r man lle mynnaf gael fy
    nghladdu

Little bird with silken feather
Golden beak and silver tongue:
There's the house, and there's the
    stable;

There's the byre with the open door
There where the great oak is growing
Is the place I'd like to be buried

Claudia Rosenzweig and Jennie Feldman
'Improvising in *ottava rima*'

On a modest stage, two poets take turns to extemporize according to a traditional pattern of rhyme and metre, their recitative-like singing full-throated, their gestures expressive. The audience is rapt, relishing the virtuosity and wondering who will falter first. These *contrasti*, contests in improvised *ottava rima*, flourish today in Italy, notably in a number of Tuscan towns, and attract a devoted following. One of the best-known is Ribolla's annual Festa della Poesia improvvisata, where themes for the contestants – put forward by the audience – can range from 'Art and Profit' to local politics. In 2009 the focus was the earthquake in Abruzzo a few days earlier, turning the event into a spontaneous elegy for the dead and bereaved.

Ottava rima, its eight hendecasyllabic (11-syllable) lines rhyming a-b-a-b-a-b-c-c, came to prominence through Boccaccio's work and the tradition of the *cantari*. It dominated Italian Renaissance poetry and early on became a favourite metre in popular culture, a way to voice life's vexations and joys, but also to celebrate poetry and song: *Se non ci fosse essa a dar conforto / Mi sembra già il mondo sarebbe morto* (If it weren't there to offer comfort / It seems to me the world would be dead).

As they alternate, each performer adopts the other's final rhyme for the first line of his (only rarely her) stanza, fitting the words to one of the traditional melodies. The *contrasti* challenge the imagination, creativity and sheer stamina of the participants, seasoned *canterini* and youngsters alike. It is also a form of skilfully crafted debate, as the participants explore public and cultural issues – celebrating, lamenting, debunking, according to the inspiration of the moment. To promote the vitality of this venerable oral tradition, which has counterparts in Corsica, Sardinia and elsewhere, the Accademia dell'Ottava in Florence offers courses and lectures on composition and improvisation in *ottava rima*.

Here are two such stanzas, from a contest between Emilio Meliani and Niccolino Grossi, in Ribolla in 2008. The first line, speaking of Bertinotti, a leader of a Leftist party, means 'I would give him my blood and also my help'.

Contrasto in ottava rima di argomento politico

io gli darei il sangue e anche il mio aiuto
se ci avesse una grave malattia
ma in politica non sono dispiaciuto
è stato ben che sia cacciato via
non son politicante tanto astuto
ma non mi tornan in conto in casa mia
da quindici anni tra discorsi e affanni
non ho fatto altro che ricever danni

c'è chi sta nelle regge chi nei capanni
chi è paladino di pur grandi imprese
però chi è attento ce l'ha vitto e panni
e a fatica arriva in fondo al mese
ora con rima e senza troppo affanni
è il popol piccolin che ce lo chiede
la sinistra 'un c'è più riman le gesta
però il problema c'è restato e resta

And here are some links, to the thing in practice:

Ottava rima - Contrasto tra Mauro Chechi e Francesco Burroni.
http://www.youtube.com/watch?v=DzEY4GUoFKk

Contrasto in ottava rima di argomento politico.
http://www.youtube.com/watch?v=-q1tN9phiUw

Canti in ottava rima sul terremoto di Abruzzo (on the earthquake
in Abruzzo).
http://www.youtube.com/watch?v=AcdbSMEXBP0

Zoltán Zelk
'Congratulatory Rhyming Telegram'
Translated from the Hungarian by
John Ridland and Peter Czipott

Zoltán Zelk (1906–81) poet and prose writer; winner of the Baumgarten (1948), Attila József (1949) and Kossuth (1953) prizes; and the Robert Graves prize for the year's most beautiful poem (1971). Avowed Communist from 1925, a willing Party hack under Stalinism until the scales fell from his eyes and he became a fervent supporter of the 1956 Revolution; imprisoned and amnestied after the Revolution.

This poem was written in response to Hungary's defeat of England, 6-3, in 1953. That match was the first international soccer match the English national team had ever lost in 90 years of play in its home stadium at Wembley. A year later, Hungary hosted a return match and won, 7-1, which is the heaviest loss the English side has ever suffered. (The lines in parentheses have been added to fill out the rhyme scheme, which Zelk left incomplete at those points.)

John Ridland and Peter Czipott

Congratulatory Rhyming Telegram
(To the 'Golden Team' of 1953)

Barely has that great victory soared, or –
SIX-THREE! – flown, across the border,

and I, tired out from cheering it on –
SIX-THREE! – preparing to lie down,

when the radio urges, 'Write a poem!'
(No need to add, in praise of *them*) . . .

Well, so I shall. Why not exult
to praise this praiseworthy result?

This triumph tells me to keep time,
speaking of it in lines of rhyme,

how heartening it was for the ear
those six Hungarian goals to hear!

And if the pompous take no pleasure?
What do they know, how dear a treasure

games can be for the full-grown man!
How every Sunday we still can

renew our childhood, which, it seems,
returns when we root for our teams . . .

For the spectator, not just tagging
along, is playing – zigging, zagging

between defenders, feinting, shooting,
wins with the team for which he's rooting –

or loses, but not now – right, friend?
As if we, on a huge grandstand,

each separate, yet all together
bend to the radio, hearing whether

Puskás completes his feinting run,
passes, and then – bad luck! this one,

Kocsis's header, bangs the crossbar,
but Bozsik comes and slams it hard!

And Hidegkuti finds the path
straight to the goal: in goes the SIXTH!

Well, so it's happened: the invitation,
matched by the zeal of my elation,

has made this verse about: SIX-THREE!
So soar away on wings of rhyme,

you telegram of congratulation:

carry our joy to the victorious
Golden Eleven, and their meritorious

managers, Mándi and Titkos both.

And carry my words, especially
to Sebes

                    (and that's all from me).

Notes: Ferenc Puskás (1927–2006), routinely counted among the top eleven footballers of all time.

Sándor Kocsis (1929–79), a member of the 'Mighty Magyars' national side of the 1950s and, along with Puskás, one of the top international goal-scorers of all time (ranked fourth; Puskás is second, Pelé third).

József Bozsik (1925–78), the deep midfielder for the Mighty Magyars.

Nándor Hidegkúti (1922–2002), a roaming midfielder-attacker for the Mighty Magyars; he scored a hat trick in the Wembley victory.

Vladislav Khodasevich
Three poems
Translated from the Russian by Peter Daniels

Vladislav Felitsianovich Khodasevich was born in Moscow in 1886, but his family were really Polish-Lithuanian and his mother was originally Jewish. Although he was russified by his education, his Polish heritage gave him a slightly oblique perspective on Russia and its poetry, alongside his deep knowledge and love of it. Being younger than Blok and the other symbolists, he rejected their methods and developed his own style with parallels to modernism in the West, rooting feelings and thoughts in precise factual description.

He left Russia in 1922 with his then partner Nina Berberova; they lived first in Berlin but then mostly in Paris, working in the exasperating Russian émigré literary world. If he had not died of liver cancer in June 1939 he would inevitably have died in Auschwitz like his widow Olga. As an émigré he was ignored or criticised by the Soviet authorities, but Nabokov considered him the finest Russian poet of the 20th century; he has now become much appreciated in Russia.

An encounter

It was morning at Santa Margherita
when I encountered her. There she stood
on the little bridge, back to the parapet, fingers
resting on the grey stone as lightly
as petals. In her white dress, vaguely
discernible, her knees were drawn together.
Waiting for someone. Who? Who is the dream
of a sixteen-year-old lovely English girl
in Venice? I don't know – and it's not for me
to know. Not for any pointless conjecture
I recollect that girl again today.
She was standing there, immersed in sunshine, but
with the soft brim of her panama touching
her slightly lifted shoulders, and the cool
shade that covered her face. Deeply blue
and pure was her gaze as it flowed out from there,
like streams of water freshly running through
the stony channel of a mountain rivulet,
melodious and swift… In that moment
I could glimpse that inexpressible look
it is our destiny as poets once
to catch, and to remember ever after.
It shows itself, a single flash before us,
godlike on earth, coming down at random
to occupy some eyes of lapis lazuli.
But they were brimming with those flaming storms,
twisting inside them were those sky-blue whirlwinds,
which reverberated then for me
in sunshine, in the splash of black gondolas,
the fleeting shadows of pigeons, and the red
flow of the wine.

And later in the evening, when I walked back
home, I was hearing whispers of the same
from the tuneful stepping of Venetian women,
and I felt my own steps more ringingly,
impetuously, lightly. Ah, but where,
where in that second did it fly away, my heart,
when the heavy key made a springy sound as
I turned it in the lock? And when I'd stepped
across the threshold of the chilly hallway,
why did I stand there by the stone cistern
in the dark, so long? Groping my way
up the staircase, being in love is what
I called this agitation. Now I realise
I had tasted strong wine that day –
and I was still feeling on my lips
that momentary taste. The eternal drunkenness
came afterwards.

13 May 1918

Note: This is one of seven blank verse poems Khodasevich wrote in
this period. Blank verse is unusual in Russian, although it had been
used by Pushkin; in Khodasevich's search for his own kind of post-
symbolist modernism he uses it for meditating on the exact meanings
of experiences. He had gone to Venice in 1911 at the age of 25,
pursuing an affair with a married woman. The affair ended, but the
experience of Venice was essential in his development; his vocation as
a poet, receptive to messages from Parnassus, was something he took
very seriously.

Ballad of the one-armed man

I think I'm going to lose my mind,
I ask myself what is the use:
a one-armed man and his pregnant wife
have gone into the picture-house.

An angel offers me the lyre,
I see the world transparently –
while he is gaping open-mouthed
at Charlie Chaplin's idiocy.

Why should he drag his little life
on such unequal terms, to live
merely a meek and unassuming
man with a folded-over sleeve?

I think I'm going to lose my mind
as pregnant wife and one-armed man
come back out of the picture-house
to walk the street for home again.

I go to fetch my leather whip
and with a long and drawn-out cry
I swing it at the angelic host,
and through the telegraph wires they fly,

bursting above the city's heights
as frightened pigeons flew above
the square in Venice once, before
the advancing footsteps of my love.

Then I approach the one-armed man,
politely taking off my hat;
I gently touch him on the sleeve
while striking up this friendly chat:

'*Pardon monsieur*, when I'm in hell
and paying for my arrogant life
with fitting punishment, and you're
in heaven with your lady wife –

floating in peaceful contemplation
over this vale of sorrowful things,
hearing celestial harmonies
and shining with your snow-white wings

– drop from your cool abode on high
one tiny feather down to me,
a snowflake falling on this breast
that's roasting for eternity.'

The one-armed man stands facing me
and offers me a little smile,
then shuffles onward with his wife,
his bowler hat on all the while.

June – 17 August 1925

Note: This poem is simply called 'Ballad' in Russian, and it harks
back to a previous 'Ballad' which I have called 'Ballad of the Heavy
Lyre (published in *PN Review*, May-June 2010). That was written in the
extraordinary winter of 1921 when Khodasevich felt himself coming
into his vocation as a poet: in it he is handed the lyre of Orpheus in a
wind that takes him far beyond his room in Petersburg. In the summer
of 1922 he left Russia and by 1925 was in Paris, where life as a poet in
exile became increasingly frustrating, and he wrote less and less.

Why ever not the four-foot iamb . . .

Why ever not the four-foot iamb,
cherished from before the flood?
And what to sing, if not to sing
the iamb's gift, so rich and good?

The angels brought it down from heights
above the stars, where Muses dwell,
more glorious than all Russia's flags,
and stronger than a kremlin wall.

Consumed by years, the names of who
had fallen at Khotín, and why,
and yet the 'Ode upon Khotín'
for us was life's initial cry.

That day a Russian muse arose
upon the snowy hills, and stood
to sing her first prodigious note
to all her distant sisterhood.

Since then in strict diversity,
as in the famous 'Waterfall',
across the same quartet of steps
the Russian verses foam and boil.

The more they spring from off the cliff,
the more the whirlpool twists away
more secret in its harmonies,
and higher leaps the sparkling spray –

that spray where, like a radiant dream
suspended joyfully in its height,
there plays chromatically with sense
the rainbow of ideal delight.

*   *   *

Its nature is mysterious,
where spondee sleeps and paeon sings,
one law is held within it – freedom.
Freedom is the law it brings . . .

1938

Note: This is the last poem Khodasevich wrote, and he left room
for another stanza in the space indicated by asterisks. The 'Ode
upon Khotín' is by Mikhail Vasilievich Lomonosov (1711–65), about
a battle against the Turks and Tatars in 1739. 'The Waterfall' is by
Gavrila Romanovich Derzhavin (1743–1816). They established the
iambic tetrameter as the classic metre of the Russian tradition, where
substituted feet are less common than in English, but I have allowed
myself some of the English kind of freedom.

Dane Zajc
Three poems
Translated from the Slovene by Angus Reid

Dane Zajc is regarded as the most important Slovene poet of the second half of the twentieth century and is, to my mind, one of the greatest 20th-century poets. Anecdote recounts that Ted Hughes was introduced to his work while on a fishing trip to Slovenia in the 1990s, and saw in Zajc's tough lyrical swing a resolution of themes than he himself had been unable to achieve. I met him at the same time, and my translations in this volume were an exchange for three translations he made of my own poetry. He was a warm and generous man: he knew all his poetry by heart and he had an extraordinary speaking voice. Born in 1929, he had a traumatic childhood, witnessing the brutal murder of his father at the hands of the occupying Nazis, who threw him into a burning house. Both of his brothers also died during the conflict. Almost all his poetry – and particularly his love poetry – reflects this experience in some way, recycling images of fire, ash and violence. Zajc only achieved official recognition at the end of his life: before then his work was banned by the communist authorities, who also forbade his enrolment at university. For four decades he worked as a city librarian, but continued to publish poetry and plays. He re-entered the public scene as a vocal supporter of the Slovenian Democratic Opposition in the late 1980s, during the Slovene Spring. Later, he served as president of the Slovene Writers Association and received the prestigious Prešeren Award for lifetime achievement. He died in 2005.

Black Flowers
(Rože Noči)

I gathered black flowers
Gathered them by night
In the hopeless meadow
In the poison light

I drank a passion drink
Drank a poison drink
Drank it seeming sweet
Sold my soul to seeming sweet
And sold my soul too cheap

Stamping on the higher slope
That black horse will have his way
He's muscled like a muscled rope
The one the devil cannot break

The force of him can force the field
And force across that meadow
The spark of him is fire-heeled
A flyer in the fire's shadow

Down the lonely length of hours
His raging ruts my head
Spattering black flowers
With blood's corrosive red

Go the Crows
(*Dva Vrana*)

Over earth frozen tight
black flight, black on white
two crows

cra cra
nae faurer can we fa

blown frozen over earth
over water frozen white
winter white

cra cra
nane ava, nane ava

black famine blown over
frozen earth, black on white
go the crows

cra cra
wing wing awa

Journeyman

(*Potepuh*)

Oh, lay my face between your paps
And drown me in your endless peace
Oh, teach me how with gentle steps
To bear myself, to make a truce

Faraway they know my name
The whisper came for me tonight
Despair and her accomplice Time
Accompany the early light

Were I to stay and stay for life
Despair would hammer her divorce
And injure this discovered love
And hollow out a lover's face

It's better to be on my way
With only here and now of you
Than to allow the prophecy
Of loveless Time to be the truth

I was never more than poor
Never wanted less than good
Never wanted more than warmth
Never kissing where I could

The love I had was never full
Until it met me at your lips
And poured a bliss into my soul
And played upon my fingertips

There's that summons in the wind
Drumming me into the open
I'm leaving it, this quiet room
This one-way conversation

Sleep. Sleep on and sleep without
My body and my fiction
I know my heart, I know my route
My worth and my addiction

Luis Rosales
From *The Trap-Net* (1980)
Translated from the Spanish by Gonzalo Melchor

Luis Rosales (1910–1992) was one of the most important voices
of the Spanish Generation of 1936 – and arguably the most
innovative Spanish poet of the second half of the twentieth
century. Although an essential figure in Spanish letters (he was
awarded the Cervantes Prize the year after Octavio Paz), his
genre-breaking works are yet to be translated into English.

The Trap-Net was published in 1980, as the first volume of
Rosales's final, longest, most ambitious and ultimately unfinished
work (a tetralogy under the title *The Complete Letter*). The book
is fashioned on Rosales's concept of 'total poetry', where lyric,
narrative, drama and the essay could all co-exist: based on a
real research trip Rosales undertook to an old fishing town in
Cádiz, the ritualistic capture of the tuna might rival the best of
Melville, and gives rise to a gripping cinematographical sequence
on life and death, power and weakness, innocence and guilt, the
witnessing and averted gaze.

In Spanish, the text bears Rosales's unique style – a blend
of surrealism, intertwined registers, anaphora and parallelism,
unusual collocations and wonderful lexical and grammatical

transgressions. His metaphors are built on a wholly personal idiom, tying line to line, poem to poem, and book to book; as the contemporary poet Vicente Gallego has written, 'all of Luis Rosales's books sound, unmistakably, like that – like Luis Rosales', and the hope of the translation is that this unique voice does, as far as possible, carry through.

THE TRAP-NET IS A CITY,
a city that is made simply of hemp rope and esparto,
a desolate and submarine city
with a long tail – it can be several kilometres long –
that rests on the coast and enters the sea,
and its role consists in guiding fish to their perdition
made up of three consecutive compartments:
the bag-net, the mid-enclosure and the chamber of death.
Due to its character of terminus in a journey of no return,
it has the shape of a labyrinth,
and,
indeed,
I must say that a trap-net
is perdition built mathematically.

NO ONE SHOULD FORGET THAT A LABYRINTH CONSISTS
    PRECISELY IN PERDITION,
and the trap-net is a labyrinth,
quite large,
made with tight nets hardened by the water,
whose walls can reach a height of up to fifty metres.
They should be defenceless, but are not;
internal currents pull at them without collapsing them;
they stay afloat with corks and are fixed to the seabed with
    anchors
– the cotter pin is the wedge that holds the bag-net
    horizontal –

and arrange themselves in such a way that they're able to
  support each other,
as their varying tightness gives them stability.
Perdition is their secret,
and the starting secret is always a labyrinth,
for the more you enter into life the more you lose yourself in
  it.
And thus
when the tuna arrive coasting the shore in search of clear
  waters,
in search of fertile, soothing and tranquil waters
where they may spawn,
the compartment doors are raised to let them in.
It is a thing well known that attraction is often deceptive,
and when the tuna enter the chamber of death,
the last door falls.
One who enters into joy is lost,
happiness only has one door which is the door of entry,
once they have passed through
they never find the exit again and the circle closes around
  their jubilation.

[. . .]

THE STREET IS A MIRACLE AND YOU FEEL IT PROPAGATING
for life is transmitted
the way a drowned man is revived when you give him your
  breath mouth to mouth.
All I needed was to gaze to feel alive as we left together
looking around us.
Yes,

I could see:

the constant eyes,
the seagulls that passed flying through the crowd with folded
      wings,
women made of mercury – it seems they touch you with their
      gaze –
and that smell of freshly-made salt piercing my bones,
that smell of salt and fish, of pepper and urine,
of ginger and sun that keeps the world on time,
and the wind like a blind man playing the violin,
and something live, ancestral, that came to us propagating:
everything was within reach
and to look was to believe because my eyes were persuaded,
I only had to open them and

                    I could see

there stood the shops with open arms,
the walls of welcoming limewash,
the limewashed walls whose whiteness seems to reach out to
      our faces,
the lack of gravity,
the children,
and the pressing windows,
and above all the pavements which are a bit transient
for in this village only one car has driven through when the
      Governor came to visit,
and now everything is known,
I don't know how,
I don't know,
but on this walk everyone shares the same gait,
and I feel the blood swinging in their bodies,
as they stumble on each other,
as they live through one another
imagined, alive, beginning.

I could see

the nets on shoulders,
the nets that have just met with the sea,
the swifts that fly chirping
and rise suddenly as if climbing up their own scream,
the doors kneeling,
the flowerpots laughing,
the bells skipping rope,
and a pensive and secondary ox,
and an old, very old woman, who approaches us to tell us:

– Hello!

and keeps looking at us once and for all
with her face of blessed rock.
There is nothing but that consecration.

I could see!

I let my gaze drive me onwards,
I let myself live,
I let myself be invaded by that shiver that makes our gazing
  eyes consanguineous
 with the world.

THE LIFE THAT BURNS IN AN INSTANT HAS A SLOW AND
  GATHERED EVOLUTION
of mineral coal that is slowly made
in its constant dormancy, as it always finds itself at the start,
and indeed,
in man the inner is mineral,
compact,
insufficient,
its essence is to burn,
it is always ready,
we never know when, but we burn.

I was, simply, enabled,
and it was twelve o'clock as we reached the tower of the trap-
    net,
we arrived silently, so as not to interrupt ourselves,
so as not to interrupt our quiet, participant and working
    contact.
The noon light dazzled the eye
when he pointed out a spot

> — *Sir, look over there?*
> *Don't you see a blanket of water that moves in a different way?*

I focused my attention and began to see:
on the surface of the sea at rest
was a square, very precise, that seemed to burble
with tiny constant shapes
like the bubbles in water when it starts to boil.
Looking on is no good
because I saw but didn't understand
the way in dreams you sometimes see, so clearly, that the sole
    of your foot becomes a dove,
and you can't walk for fear of hurting it.

> — *Notice the different shapes that heave the water?*
> *It is the chamber of death and there must be forty tuna in it.*
> *I was counting them before.*

> — *How can you count something underwater?*

> — *It takes a while to learn but you do,*
> *for every so often the tuna get restless,*
> *and when they move they stir up the sea,*
> *you just have to count their movements to know their number.*

> — *Don't you worry about making mistakes?*

— I can't make mistakes. This is my trade.
Tomorrow I will raise the nets and you'll be able to check.
Tomorrow is the great day.

'It won't be for me,' I thought,
and a stray smile was left on my mouth,
unpursing it,
the way we fold a handkerchief exactly on the right place.

[...]

AT FOUR IN THE MORNING THE NIGHTWATCHMAN CAME
   LOOKING FOR ME
with a lamp on his shoulder and his stick pealing at the door.
When I came out on the street a testamentary gloom was in
   the air,
and I reached the shore as the sailors pushed their boats off
   the sand,
and made them pitch jumping quickly over the gunwale,
and balanced them with their weight as they set out to sea.
There is nothing more silent than an oar entering the water,
nothing more sensual,
and more nocturnal
than an oar that breaks water and penetrates its depths,
and makes us feel that extremely deep beat that quivers only
   at the end of the blade,
until rhythm turns into caress and makes the effort
   stimulating, uniform and unisonous.
The voice keeps the stroke in time
and slowly turns into song.

                    'I don't sing my song
                    but to those who are with me.'

And I don't know who is with me,
while the sailors sing the romance of Gerineldos
— the page boy is sleeping on the sea with the sword at his
    side —
and the monotonous romance has ragged interpolations,
and the words sound at times like lips and at times like
    tatters,
but they're all sewn by a single thread that keeps the voices at
    the same distance,
and I see that rhythm is prior to the sea and unites it,
and I see that rhythm is prior to man and engenders him,
and in truth it is so because I'm seeing
the waves and the boats and the voices in the friendly society
    of a frontier,
of a frontier that enters far into the sea and spreads out.

[...]

THE SINGING OF THE CREWS HAD ALREADY CEASED AND
    ALL GAZES CONVERGED ON A SINGLE POINT,
just as pupils, when they gaze intently, will contract.
From the surrounding boats everyone watched the harpooners
who were bent over to reach their prey
with their feet on the nets and their whole body over the
    gunwale,
holding on to the stays with one hand
and the other, the right one, gloved with the gaff.
(A grey glove, made of plush, with a hook between index and
    thumb,
not too large as it is only six centimetres long,
which suffice.)
The harpooners must focus their life onto that single hand,
and wait as the tuna in one of their quick and disparate turns
pass almost brushing them
and then
they make a dexterous and extremely fast move

a— a swipe —
and hook their prey by the gullet.
It must be there,
precisely,
and I was watching it,
and each tuna can weigh, easily, more than three hundred
     kilos,
and in a single moment it is held in the air by a small, gloved
     hand.
It is impossible and so simple,
when the tuna feels wounded it gathers strength again,
to charge at the air,
and the harpooner then takes advantage of the jump
to make it change direction and let it fall on the bilge.

THERE IS SOMETHING BULLFIGHTER-LIKE IN HIS GESTURE
for he turns his body slowly and deftly until he lets the fish
     go in the void,
and I was watching it,
and the tuna is still so alive in the moment of falling that the
     urge to live sharpens its fall,
then it lies tossing its head on the hold
in colloquial death,
in a death still spoken,
with that dilated movement the body has when it expires.
The sun, the air, the rhythm of that virile and merciless
     ritual,
bloody and beautiful, mysterious and sad,
till the water in the ring cleared again,
and was left tightened like a scream,
lightly coloured by the blood of the tuna.
And I was left alone between death and the morning, I'm not
     sure why, faced with that scream,
and I began to feel the air between my vertebrae,
the air between my bones pulling them apart;

it was air with no light, an in-between-cold that advanced in
    me,
and that is all,
I can't say any more,
like wet paper my body folded last-but-one and fallen,
nothing within me held me up.

Kerry Featherstone
Five poems from Ingrid Thobois' novel
Le Roi d'Afghanistan ne nous a pas mariés

I met Ingrid Thobois at the Fête de l'Humanité. We found that
we had several interests and writers in common (Bruce Chatwin,
Nicolas Bouvier). I had already published an essay on travel writing
in Afghanistan, and was teaching a module on representations
of Afghanistan. I read her novel, *Le Roi d'Afghanistan ne nous a
pas mariés*, and wanted my students to read it, but there was no
translation available. Over coffee a year or so later, I suggested
to Ingrid that I should translate it. She replied that it would be
a 'beau projet'.

I write poetry in French and English, sometimes in the same
poem. As I worked through the prose translation, some sections
seemed to stand out as having an intensity of language that felt
like poetry: brilliant visual imagery and a balance of commitment
and detachment. There are moments of reflection as well as the
detailed observation often associated with writing about place.
The whole novel is written in a series of short episodes, so this
also suggested the possibility of some sections being 'translated'
into stand-alone pieces. I started work on two of these: Ingrid
liked them. The process feels like collaboration: the dialogue
between author and translator is important.

Then I started to be concerned with questions of ownership and authority: as I pulled out the sections, I was working on line endings, omitting phrases, changing the order of images and events. How far could I go, and still claim that an act of translation was taking place? Is there a clear line between translation and found poetry? These questions formed the basis of a paper at the Nottingham University 'It Gives Us the Other' conference on poetry in translation early in 2011.

The translation of the novel is now finished, and in search of a publisher. The poems printed here mark the start of what I hope will be an ongoing practice: as well as my own bilingual poems, I am alert to the idea that translation across form as well as language is a fruitful source of new writing.

Spark Up The Sky

See the skill of the ironworker
hit saucepan handles
and understand
– with a few blows of a hammer –
what little you really have need of.
These gestures are silent elsewhere.

So I turn what I see of this
into rhythm: I hear craftsmanship speak.
And Afghanistan sticks
to my skin: where everything is made
with ten fingers and a bunch of nothing.

Wherever one man is working, there are ten others
in the press:
when cutting up beef he is not to be left alone.
And one lifts the tail, another the left leg;
a third flushes the blood with tubs of water.

But you also meet kite-flyers, who spark up the sky.
And the counters of clouds
whose only tool is the eye: you see
them in their great age.
And observers can be counted in dozens,
posted at the corners;
a startled air at having been passed
by so many children and so much dust.

The Great Mystery (Ingrid Thobois' Power Cut)

The electricity has not come back to my place:
round here you don't ask for that kind of miracle.
You have to wait for God
to give
what God is going to give.
Is an old ancestral error overriding
the relationship between the Almighty
and my meter readings?
My generator, choking under the voltage demands of
a single kettle,
has chosen this moment
to cough a cloud of steam into my face.
Quickly: empty it! Or fill it up?

*   *   *

If only I'd known which,
blood or ink,
was supposed to feed the other.
Heart or print-cartridge: the great mystery
of the pump, so fearful
when nothing will power itself any more.
As long as the day
wants so little from us, we hang onto what's left
of our body:
new lungs for a cigarette,
the barely-dulled picture that the mirror sends
of our discomfort.

*   *   *

The week before, in the same mirror,
in profile with an arched back,
I had invented . . .
a little child making my belly round.
And had believed
in love, with more force than a holy man can believe in his
    cross.
Anyone can make a mistake.

Ingrid Thobois in the Market at Kabul

Tarpaulin slaps in the shifting wind
and fine dust swirls up columns of light.
Tiny boutiques are shading bolts of slumping cloth.
A stall-holder disappears, bent
below four long yards of fabric,
from which one sandal sticks out.
Lethargy leans on the bazaar. The alley
of spices is hidden. Perched on their stalls,
the men watch my steps.
Saffron, cumin, cardamom, white pepper:
the spices form little multicoloured dunes, as
the merchant, out of the love of making it beautiful,
has fused the colours of fire.

I turn and come upon a passage
that is too narrow for traffic:
I sneak into the density of unexpected silence.
A brief loss of balance.
Carpets of almonds, fig necklaces,
mountains of shrivelled grapes.
The heat intensifies the smell
of concentrated sugar.
In the blue shadows, the tiny contours
of the dried fruit weave a perfect landscape.
Suddenly the eye is overcome, can make out
nothing more: I stumble out into a noisy alleyway,
boiled as the sun hurls itself
at pewter kettles which are ready
to fly away on the slightest breath of wind.

Everything melts in the day as it drags on.
Then the moment when the wind gets up:
it will soon blow in violent gusts.
A veil of dust clouds my view, and the women
wearing chadors disappear in floating blue cloth.
It's my favourite time, when everything is
uncertain, from the world that surrounds me
to my presence in it. It's the hour when I tremble,
when the vagabond spirit invents legends.
Three drops of rain, a handful of melancholy,
and the desire to huddle into arms whose warmth
will leave no doubt. This evening I find it so difficult
to tell the sky from the earth.

In Qalai Fatullah, the most peaceful district,
it's as if the dustmen, bakers, schoolchildren,
and fruit sellers had all spread the word:
behind the painted corrugated-iron door lives a foreigner.
everyone knows *The Little Blue Door*,
from the bookseller, with his forgotten riches,
to the postman who comes with mail
that would have been lost elsewhere: from the other side of
     town
'For the French teacher, *The Little Blue Door*,
Qalai Fatullah, Kabul, Afghanistan.'

Crossing the Chador

Languages, lands: that means frontiers.
To imagine, to hide behind, or cross.
Only spectres know
the formless interiors that unwind,
where it only takes a fist,
pulled back or offered,
to release bliss or thunder.

In Afghanistan these lines are rarely rubbed out,
however badly they are drawn.
A shout in your face, or a pretty woman
lifting her chador and allowing the light to play
over her expression says that
you've crossed.

Here are shadows: curves of thin shoulders.
The breeze blowing cloth, which would be carried away
if someone didn't watch out. Wide, with
infinite flowing folds, the chador walks
an agonising waltz. Twos, threes;
they ghost across the broken surface as cars rush by.
Slow, one hand at a parting guesses
what the world holds in wait.
But the opening is tight and grilled with thread.

For the beggar-woman of the streets,
Ramadan is not devotion; it's daily bread.
And God doesn't give equal shares for breaking
the fast when night comes

Nameless sculptures crouch under blue pleats,
domed mounds hold out their hands.
Darkness, except when light
pierces the mesh, uncovering an iris, its colour.

I have called for the miracle: I have prayed for a face, and it
    has come.
With humour and grace beyond form she throws
a panel of her chador into the sky,
and sees me in her fortune-teller's tent.

There is sudden life.
Fortresses of cloth as light as the wind, so easy to lift,
so rarely taken off. She has eyes,
a radiant face, skin that asks to be caressed
and bare arms in a T-shirt
stamped with little 'hellos' in rows.
Now that the indigo frontier has been rolled back, I discover
a body the same as mine . . . a name.

Fariba's voice is low and echoes in the blue.
Less than thirty, stomach rounded by a child
and she laughs as she outlines
life with agile fingers, sparkling her eyes.
Fariba, asking my name, reminding me of hers:
clear laughter, a hand on her throat.

While a mirror with no silvering hides
all women,
while thousands of bodies
have the appearance of one, there is only shape.
Fariba's irritated hand pushes off her chador:
free under a rain of stars.
I swallow breath.
She shows no relief.

She chases hair from copper-coloured cheeks:
I watch her, distracted by her ease.
Eyebrows lower, lift and arch.
Lips purse and then relax.
Fariba forgets her uncovered face.
Sometimes the start
of a question crosses her eyes.

So she disappears, still holding my hand,
in the eye of her cape's elegant whirlpool.
Across the material, her deaf words still reach me
and I read her smile as if it's transparent,
trying to find something in her blue form
that will allow me to recognise her walk tomorrow:
a tiny detail that would allow me to
take her hand because I recognise her.

At the corner of the next street
a man is offended
at her face opened to a young foreigner.
Fariba is far off: she has been wiped away.
I can do nothing for her.
She is begging after her day job.
The hospital doesn't pay much.
Her husband is dead: he will never know
the child that draws a curve across her chador
when the head-wind outlines all those beautiful contours.

Fariba, I never realised
that a chador
could be lifted so
naturally.

The Writing Scorpion

Four days now past,
a white scorpion thicker than a rubber,
longer than my little finger,
has insisted on surviving
under this glass.
I am experimenting, to see if the rumour is true that
arthropods commit suicide
I am pitiless.

It's completely false.
And my beast, starved, and with no more than a thimble of
    air,
continues to grow.
To a point that makes me scared.
I'm thinking of letting it go, unless tonight
(and I'd be surprised),
it finally consents.
I work as if there was no problem: I scry the outside world,
and my scorpion is of precious help.

He hasn't noticed that my experiment
(with killing risk),
proves that I am paying attention;
giving back his dignity.
He will die as no other scorpion:
I'll have counted the phrases of vertebrae,
I'll have searched for words to describe colour
(and the sweet curve of his pincers);
I'll have called his tail a pretty question mark.

I don't like him, but four days he's been fuelling my work.

Lutz Seiler
Five poems
Translated from the German by
Alexander Booth

Lutz Seiler, considered one of Germany's most interesting and singular contemporary poets, was born in 1963 in Gera, a town in the eastern part of the state of Thuringia in the former German Democratic Republic. In the early 1960s this area was one of the world's main centres of uranium mining and was ravaged by it. When the mining ceased, the inhabitants of the surrounding areas were relocated. Seiler trained as a mason and a carpenter and completed mandatory military service. After studying in Halle and Berlin, in 1997 he became the literary director of the Peter Huchel Museum, outside Potsdam, the most recent in a line extending from the poet Huchel himself (who permanently left the GDR in 1971) to the poet and translator Erich Arendt.

Lutz Seiler has published half a dozen volumes of poetry, short stories and essays. His many prizes include the Dresden Poetry Prize (2000), the Bremen Prize for Literature (2004), the Ingeborg Bachmann Prize (2007), and, most recently, the Fontane Prize (2010). He was writer-in-residence at the German Academy in Rome in 2010 and at the Villa Aurora in Los Angeles in 2003. In addition, he has been elected a member of the Saxon Academy of the Arts, Dresden, and the Academy of Arts, Berlin.

From *in field latin*

everything about me

there was a time when very slowly
with my ears from out
of the rain i came, saw rain
& could think of rain.

like oil gods
the old motors would crawl
out behind the hill &
the harvest began. i

would stick my arms deep
into the grain, would press
the seeds between my fingers &
had to close my eyes.

down from the beam hung a thin
skim of fat, upon which the dead
flies slept &

in the hollow mould of the walls
hovered a child who
would call on me. he knew
everything about me

the stay

one evening they came
the dead of my house
back from the train-station. one

after the other, with
balled fists, reminiscent
of tulips in their

night-reserve, reminiscent,
in the long being-dead, of all
the wasted time. from way back now

all's been theirs: every word, just
out of the lips, every good
sentence, as always

the home-made liverwurst, the
plum preserves, and in addition
all the cigarettes and whatever

alcohol within reach. ceaselessly
they watched tv, ate chocolate (in huge
amounts) & whispered

verses to themselves. one evening
they came the dead of my house
back from the train-station. it was december &

their next train did not leave till march

autumn

is silence & custom. autumn
is rake, wood, is a mild
chill upon the eyes &

unexpected gooseflesh. is also
the good old ready-to-fight feeling, soft, secret, skull-still
maturing designs. the leaves all burnt, sand

still warm beneath the ashes, you
feel it now upon your hand: something
wants to flee & something never to leave. so

one simply goes all the way
out back, behind the house. one falls
onto the grass and looks around:

globe-illumination, earth-rotation
across the neighbours' balconies. once
home & return

it glistens from the dog-chains. 'my god
how the pine-tree tips are
all of a sudden red up top!' & under the earth

lie the dead
& hold the ends of the roots in their mouths

along i went, i froze

along i went (in the woods), i felt
skin upon my head & a fine
abrasion of tide about my ears were

i another man…how quickly
all just thought again
forgot within the underbrush once i was

another: in hydesville, missouri
born. my daughter dolores
liked to clap her hands, she clapped & clapped &

one day something clapped back:
his name was splitfoot. dead
five years before – 'another man'

so ran the theme of this going – hard
in the ether, soft in the ear, good material
for those at home at their poems, but also

for all those who alone
(so damn alone)
are outside there & listen

inventory

you've investigated time
in the lampshade: branches, two building-
rows, already dusted off word by word.
all is open up to the eyes – who

said that? i sit here now as if
written myself, pencil on
paper. the gas meter ticks, one
drinks oneself tight for this text & has

the wrong punctuation in the blood. over there
the bottles on the oven, here
the wood chips, half chewed to bits, the smell
of the freshly sawn – every

character scrapes the things
back into your bones through graphite, only
it never occurs to you to cry

Stephen Watts
Three poems after Tudor Arghezi

Tudor Arghezi (1880–1967, born in Bucharest of peasant stock) was one of the great European poets of the first half of the C20th, managing to melt symbolist experience in with raw folk outbursts. Michael Impey wrote that 'no poet of the modern world . . . has treated the motif of spiritual exile with such pathos, or grappled so unavailingly with the problem of human imperfection.' He lived through two wars and as many home-grown totalitarian regimes. His best work is included in his first book *Fitting Words* (*Cuvinte potrivite* 1927), in *Flowers Of Mildew* (*Flori de mucigai* 1931), in *Evening Verses* (*Versuri de seara* 1935) and in *One Hundred and One Poems* (*Una suta une poeme* 1947).

These are very much 'versions' and I've given myself more 'air' than I might in other translations. 'Rada' and 'Tinca' are both from *Flori de mucigai*, while 'Corrupt words' is based on the poem 'Cuvinte stricate' (from *Versuri de seara*) with echoes from the title poem of *Flori de mucigai* and other texts. With all three 'translations' I was trying for the *sound* of Arghezi's poetry, because it seems to me that is what is most intricately fused into the greatness of his work and what is also most easily missed when translating him.

I owe much to Michael Impey and Brian Swann's very fine translations in their bilingual *Selected Poems Of Tudor Arghezi* (Princeton University Press 1976), but I also looked at other, sometimes badly literal, translations in various anthologies and other sources. I kept the context of the Romanian originals always in mind, as if to *read* the poet's sound and to *hear* it back in English. I wrote these versions in the 1980s (then lost them for 20 years together with a batch of my own poems) and would like to publish them now in tribute to the deeply original music of a great Romanian poet.

Rada

With a flower in her teeth
Rada is a wreath
of hot-thorned roadside roses
dancing in the rain-soaked soil.
She crouches, jumps, hoops her hands
she fritters joining-ropes of gold
and turns them into bridle-bits of foam.
She stoops her stiff back low
then bends her hip to throw her leg right back
toward the sky-flown starling flock
that's trapped silver in its star rack.

While jumping she had let us see
her flower, her red-black peony.
It seems the box that holds her stone of blood
was opened & then fell shut again. I would
like to bring my mouth down there & suck . . .

I would like to nail
her amber statue, as a blacksmith
does fillies lying on the ground
that too moaned when they were downed.

Aiee, mother, tell her not to dance
or make water lilies of her flesh
or willows seeded by horse & chance.
I am ill with scent too strong for me
I'm sick with song that makes me groan,
Mother, do not let her dance – or, no –
let her come & dance & lie & moan.

Tinca

Her hip-basket of
sunlight propped on her thigh,
her pannier of sheaves with yellow
eyes & lashes, her milky
flowers & night carnations,
her breasts & their black berries
tricked men's angel pride, her cries
'who'll buy flowers off the bride?'

Tell us, Tinca, tell
silky slippers, earrings, beaded ease,
Năstase didn't give you all these,
and every ring on every finger
did Năstase put all of them there?

So who did you let knead your ebony flesh
drinking back your fake, derisive sighs?
Who did you lie down with, threshing
the royal form of your formless thighs?

Who loosed your hair, stinking of smoke,
and pulled away your stockings & your slip?
Who was it buried your crazy, crackling head
with buckled sinews & arms about what bed
then shivered quietness to your bone of bones?

You never would tell anyone
where you spent your nights, you sweet-
smelling girl selling May gentians.

And now Năstase's inside for life.
He did only penetrate you the once but he
went right through to the shaft of his knife.

Corrupt Words

All my
words are crooked,
awry scrawls, got so dead
drunk they have to crawl,
far away when near at hand,
slumped, got up, sumped down again,
wanting to run with energy
but lolled around the floors,
crackle, kink, are erratic, shrill
too much laughter's made them ill.

They got corrupted on their own.
They ran through swamps on gala days
hoping to get to the holiday zone –
my mildew flowers & fairground sprays
the daubed signs of my blunt claws.

Don't touch my words any more.
Don't let your lips move easily
on hissing sound. Nothing's proved.
Soar. Or sour. Or seer. Or sore.
Don't bring them here for song or
pamper them with rhymed music.

Gobshite ! They make me sick.

Anthony Rudolf
Two extracts from *Silent Conversations: A Reader's Life*

The title of John Adlard's short study of Apollinaire's London phase, *One Evening of Light Mist in London*, is taken from the first line of 'La Chanson du mal aimé', a wondrous love poem for Annie Playden, the one woman known to have escaped the old rogue's embraces, by emigrating to Texas from Landor Road in Stockwell, south London. (Had Apollinaire heard of Walter Savage Landor? He would have been struck by the irony of a street named after a poet one of whose most famous poems includes the lines: 'A night of memories and sighs / I consecrate to thee'. Mind you, one night is quite a short period.) There are other poems about Annie: 'L'Émigrant de Landor Road' and 'Annie': I inspected 75 Landor Road some years ago, when attending a session at an acupuncturist's, three doors away. Half a century after she fled, Playden, interviewed by Professor Leroi Breunig, said: 'Kostro [he was born Kostrowicki], what became of him?' Here is my copy of Oliver Bernard's *Selected Poems* of Apollinaire, which contains a long letter, dated 17 March 1986, in his beautiful italic hand, about a poem we had both translated, and the letter I wrote him after reading a review of his translations. We would meet years later on the Rimbaud-Verlaine London house committee and at Michael Hamburger's funeral, when I recited the Kaddish in a country church. Running to catch the metro which would take me to the Eurostar after Yves Bonnefoy's daughter's wedding reception at the Maison de l'Amérique latine in the summer of 2007, I saw again the plaque marking Apollinaire's apartment in Boulevard Saint-Germain and made a mental note to return to the wonders of his poetry, although I am ashamed to say I did not realise (until put right by Claude Vigée) that there is a pun on Loup in the ferocious love poems addressed to Lou.

I have fond memories of a playful, crazy and difficult epic novel with an exotic title, each long chapter consisting of one paragraph. I bought *Grabinoulor* by Pierre Albert-Birot in 1964, when its abridged version was published. On its first appearance, in 1919, it was championed by Apollinaire, Max Jacob and Céline. According to Jacob's blurb, Albert-Birot was chatting with the poet about his concept, 'surnaturalism': 'it's the wrong word.' 'All right,' said Apollinaire, 'let's change it to "surrealism."' (He may also have known that Nerval uses the word 'super-naturalism' in respect of dreams.) According to James Williams's *Cocteau*, however, Apollinaire coined the word for *Parade*, which Cocteau created for Diaghilev and the Ballets Russes in 1917, with sets by Picasso and music by Satie. On the other hand, Jonathan Wilson, in *Marc Chagall*, tells us that Apollinaire coined the word (again in 1917) after seeing the painter's 'Hommage to Apollinaire'. Peter Cook has a wonderful surrealist sketch (which I found on the Net) about the stone-age man who invented the bandambladastiddle: he had much less success than his neighbour, whose identical invention was called the wheel. What fun, therefore, to find in Mark Ford's essay on Breton in *A Driftwood Altar* that, one month later, Apollinaire subtitled his own play, *Les Mamelles de Tirésias*, 'a surrealist drama' and offered this explanation of the term: 'when man tried to imitate walking he created the wheel, which does not resemble a leg. He then performed an act of surrealism without realising it.'

Join *MPT* at 'Poetry Parnassus'
Southbank Centre, 26ᵗʰ June – 1ˢᵗ July 2012

Tuesday 26ᵗʰ June, 7pm, Poetry Parnassus Launch
7pm, Purcell Room, Queen Elizabeth Hall
Tickets £8

Kristiina Ehin will launch her *MPT Poets* pamphlet 'The Final Going of Snow', translated by Ilmar Lehtpere, during the opening event of the festival. Zeyar Lynn and Alvin Pang will also launch their new collections, and Simon Armitage will open the festival with an introduction to *The World Record*, a landmark international anthology with poems from over 200 countries.

Wednesday 27th June
Launch of *MPT* 3/17 'Parnassus'
Introduced by David and Helen Constantine
8pm, Saison Poetry Library

Every issue of *MPT* in the third series has been an anthology of languages, voices, and topics – world-wide and from different ages. Our latest issue 'Parnassus' continues that tradition, with the abundant contribution of poets and translators invited to Southbank Centre for the Cultural Olympiad. We are proud to present some of them this evening. This event is the idea and spirit of the magazine in practice.

Admission free but space is limited.
To book your place email specialedition@poetrylibrary.org.uk

Sunday 1ˢᵗ July
Ted Hughes Celebration Reading
12 noon, Purcell Room, Queen Elizabeth Hall
Tickets £8

Christopher Reid, Simon Armitage and David Constantine celebrate the life and work of Ted Hughes, co-founder of *MPT*, with readings of his translations, letters and biography, and of his own poems in Belarusian, French, Greek and Turkish. This event is in partnership with *Modern Poetry in Translation*.

Sunday 1ˢᵗ July
Modern Poetry in Translation Third Series Retrospective
Presented by David and Helen Constantine
3pm, Clore Ballroom, Royal Festival Hall
Free (no need to sign up in advance)

In 17 issues since the launch of the third series of *MPT* in the summer of 2004 David and Helen Constantine have continued in the spirit of Ted Hughes and Daniel Weissbort, who founded *MPT* in 1965. With readings by a range of contributors to the third series they will show at least a little of the variety of the publications: the many countries, cultures, languages, different centuries. Also the many ways in which they have understood the word 'translation'. And something also of their social and political concerns.

Book ticketed events at the Southbank Centre Ticket Office: 0844 847 9910
Book online www.southbankcentre.co.uk/poetryparnassus

Poets on the South Bank

Algeria – Adel Guémar

Armenia – Razmik Davoyan

Estonia – Kristiina Ehin

Ethiopia – Bewketu Seyoum

Georgia – Maya Sarishvili

Haiti – Évelyne Trouillot

Iceland – Gerður Kristný
Photo: Kristinn Ingvarsson

Latvia – Kārlis Vērdiņš

Luxembourg – Anise Koltz

Malta – Immanuel Mifsud
Photo: Melvin Mifsud

Mauritania – Mbarka Mint al-Barra'
Photo: Poetry Translation Centre

Mongolia – Hadaa Sendoo

Nepal – Yuyutsu RD Sharma

Somalia – Abdullahi Botan,
Rob Inglis and Hoppa!

South Korea – Kim Hyesoon

Sudan – Al-Saddiq Al-Raddi
*Photo: Crispin Hughes, Poetry
Translation Centre*

Chinese Taipei – Chen Li

Anna Selby
Poetry Parnassus

"'Energy is eternal delight," said Blake, and surely delight involves variety. There is no one coat that fits all poets, thank heaven' (George Szirtes).

When I was a child, I used to spend hours playing a computer game called Toejam and Earl. In the game, you'd explore strange countries. When you first began, it was a mass of blue squares, then as you walked the squares would disappear one by one to reveal a new land. With Poetry Parnassus, it has taken over a year, rather than hours and the 204 countries have been revealed to me by the generosity of strangers.

The research has been my greatest lesson in Geography: I can now give you directions to San Marino, American Samoa and The Federated States of Micronesia with ease, or provide a guided tour of the spoken word scene in the Pacific islands. It has been a process of discoveries: uncovering poetic traditions, politics and regions through their keenest observers. My nights have been spent reading Romanian prose poetry, morning commutes filled with the rhythms of Arabic verse and lunch breaks sat in the Saison Poetry Library exploring Island poems from places that are blue dots on atlases.

My findings have not just been poets, but the most inventive array of publications, festivals and projects: including silent poetry slams, poetry karaoke and even a poetry laundrette, where you have to unbutton shirts to read the poems written on the inside of them. One of the most inspiring collectives I found was Casagrande: a group of poets who met through the Chilean equivalent of the Eric Gregory Awards. One of the things they created was an invisible magazine, where each page was broadcast on national radio. They were in their kitchen one day, listening to page 14 (which was birdsong) when they noticed the birds outside were responding to the calls, then they found the same thing was happening in the next neighbourhood, and the next and they realised they'd made all the birds of Chile sing. They published another issue of the magazine with letters from school children to the stars, which they sent into space with a Chilean astronaut. The first letter they received said: Please can you leave the stars on in the day? Casagrande will be at Poetry Parnassus Festival as they are the creators of *Rain of Poems*, a breathtaking sight in which 100,000 poems (all in translation) are dropped from a helicopter. When they did it in Berlin in 2010, 8000 people gathered and leaped up to catch the poems as they fell, or shook them from the trees, the different poems became currency with people exchanging them, until not a single one was left. This same event is planned for the opening ceremony of Poetry Parnassus with poems by 304 poets in languages ranging from Gun to Kyrgyz.

From the beginning, I wanted the world to help decide which poets should be part of the festival, so set it up so that anyone anywhere could suggest up to three poets online (their gold, silver and bronze choice, in order of preference). We had over 6000 suggestions of poets, griots, spoken-word artists, praise singers, rappers and storytellers and we have tried to reflect this in the choices we've made, so that we can celebrate the full range of ways people work with words.

In Greek mythology, Parnassus was a mountain sacred to Apollo. It became known as the home of the Muses. Today, poets don't tend to gather on mountains, but each international festival is its own Parnassus, its own bringing together of writers and thinkers, its own offering to people to come and learn.

Poetry Parnassus is part of the Southbank Centre's Festival of the World, which takes its inspiration from Pierre de Coubertin, a man who in 1890 visited my sleepy hometown of Much Wenlock, where a doctor called William Penny Brookes was so tired of everyone being drunk that in 1850 he had set up the Olympian Games; for the 'moral, physical and intellectual improvement' of the local population. After Poetry Parnassus, some of the poets will be following in Pierre de Coubertin's footsteps and heading to Much Wenlock as part of a national tour. The world will be coming to London this Summer, I hope you can meet them. If you have your diary to hand, please jot in these dates: 26th June – 1st July. I'd love to welcome you to the Southbank Centre so you can make your own discoveries.

Anna Selby

Programmer for Poetry Parnassus

Literature and Spoken Word Co-ordinator,
Southbank Centre

Kārlis Vērdiņš
Four poems
Translated from the Latvian by Ieva Lešinska

The poet, critic and translator Kārlis Vērdiņš was born in 1979 in Riga and graduated in cultural theory from the Latvian Academy of Culture. Vērdiņš has a PhD in Literature from the University of Latvia (2009). Since 2007, he has been working at the Institute of Literature, Folklore and Art of the University of Latvia. Vērdiņš is also a member of the editorial team of the literary magazine *Latvju Teksti*.

He is the author of three poetry collections – *Ledlauži* (The Icebreakers, 2001), *Biezpiens ar krējumu* (Cottage Cheese with Cream, 2004) and *Es* (Me, 2008). Vērdiņš' poetry has been translated into several languages and included in the anthology of young poets from Central and Eastern Europe *A Fine Line* (Arc Publications, 2004) and *Six Latvian Poets* (Arc Publications, 2011). Translations of his poems have been collected in separate volumes in Russian (2003), Polish (2009) and Czech (2012, forthcoming) as well as in various anthologies and magazines.

Vērdiņš has translated the works of T.S. Eliot, Walt Whitman, Emily Dickinson, Georg Trakl, Joseph Brodsky, Konstantin Biebl and other European and American poets, including Russian poets of Latvia.

His publications on literature include monographs *The Social*

and Political Dimensions of the Latvian Prose Poem (Pisa, 2010) and
Bastarda forma (Riga, 2011).

In 2001 and 2008, he received the newspaper Diena Culture
Award; in 2006, the Copyright Infinity Award. Vērdiņš' is also a
recipient of the Poetry Prize 2008 (for *Me*) and Annual Literary
Award 2007 for his book of children's verse, *Alphabet Soup*.

Bon appétit!

If you knew what's in that hot dog,
you would certainly not eat it.
If you knew how that plate was washed,
you would certainly not lick it clean.
If you knew who sewed your jacket
and how its sales rights were obtained,
you would certainly not wear it.
If your mother knew,
who will take off your jacket tonight,
she might not have even borne you.

If you knew where my mouth may have strayed,
you would certainly not kiss me.
If you knew what my mouth has said,
you would certainly not listen.
So eat your hot dog, button up your jacket,
let's go ahead and pay and go to my place.
What I can say to you in all sincerity
takes just a couple of words: bon appétit!

Victory

Let's play a game in which you could win!
Table tennis would do,
as would orienteering in the Kalngale forest.
We can compare our weenies or shots we have downed –
I am ready to accept your rules.

I'd like to see the smile,
that would brighten your face after the victory.
I'd like to see how you fall asleep, satisfied,
leaving me sleepless –
me, who upon hearing 'victory', 'achievement', 'success',
just shudders with disgust.

Dusting

The space around me shed its former skin,
and it collected in the corners as whirls of dust.
The space lives on without remembering.
I try to learn from it: I pick up the dust,
take a shower, rub off old skin.

The new pink, moist skin remembers nothing.
How else could I be sitting in that same room,
sleeping in that same bed, taking that same shower,
rubbing myself with those same hands.

Otherwise I would have to drop down in the corner,
turn to dust, end up in a black plastic sack,
wait for a Tuesday or a Saturday
when the garbage truck would come
to put me in a container and then drive on
to these same familiar streets.

I sleep in that same bed,
my forehead like a freshly swept floor,
my skin like a pink pillow-case,
and I remember nothing.

Adults

'Close your mouth,' say the adults, 'you're getting soup all
    over your shirt!'
They wipe my lips in a greasy towel and mutter:
other kids your age eat on their own,
they clean themselves and know to say 'thank you',
with other kids your age one can tell who takes after whom.

Feed me, adults,
you who eat with such agility and much.
When I grow up, I will study law and accounting,
I will play the violin, chess and tennis – whatever will make
    you happy,
just do not raise your voices.

'Close your mouth,' say the adults, 'and listen up:
when you cross that second bridge, toss in the wreath,
then serve the meat pies, give schnapps to the adults,
   lemonade to kids.
Then you will go through a gate and balloons will be
   released.
Don't run ahead of everyone, smile!'

Feed me, adults, you who know more about those bridges.
Aunts and uncles from both sides,
colleagues, friends and classmates,
all will have a chance to come up with good wishes.
It will take long, happy years to make them all come true.

'Close your mouth,' say the adults,
'lie down, let's take your blood pressure.
If you get close to the stove one more time,
if you try to fry something there one more time,
we'll send you elsewhere and you'll be fed by strangers!'

Feed me, adults, I no longer remember your names,
yet I recognize every feature in your cross faces.
For many long years I listened and learned,
there is much I could tell you now,
yet the spoons keep getting in the way –

interrupted mid-word, I swallow it all unsaid,
with my mouth half-open, my mouth full of wonders.

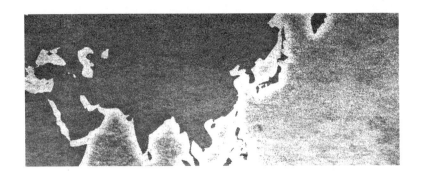

Kim Hyesoon
Three poems
Translated from the Korean by Don Mee Choi

Kim Hyesoon is one of the most prominent contemporary poets of South Korea. She lives in Seoul and teaches creative writing at the Seoul Institute of the Arts. Kim was one of the first few women to be published in the literary journal, *Munhak kwa jisông* [Literature and Intellect]. During the 1970-80s, this journal and *Ch'angjak kwa pip'yông* [Creation and Criticism] were the two leaders of the intellectual and literary movement against the U.S.-backed military dictatorships. Kim's poetry gained prominence from the late 1990s. She was the first woman to receive prestigious awards such as Kim Su-yông Literary Prize, Contemporary Poetry Award, and Midang Poetry Prize. Kim's poetry in translation can be found in *When the Plug Gets Unplugged* (Tinfish, 2005), *Anxiety of Words* (Zephyr, 2006), and *Mommy Must Be a Fountain of Feathers* (Action Books, 2008), and *All the Garbage of the World, Unite!* (Action Books, 2011).

Sunstroke

Get submerged
Get submerged in the blazing sun
Get submerged in the rippling blazing sun
Hear something as I get submerged in the rippling blazing
sun
Hear something then don't hear then hear again as I get
submerged in the rippling blazing sun
It's like the voice of someone confessing while shaking softly
boiling sand
It's the voice I have wanted to hear for a thousand years
Hear something then don't hear then hear again then don't
again as I get submerged in the rippling blazing sun
Lie down
Lie down on the floor of the blazing sun
Lie down on the cold floor of the blazing sun
It is so hot that the cold floor of the blazing sun sweats
The sweat of the cold floor of the blazing sun is like a knife
blade
Among the knife-like drops of sweat from the cold floor of
the blazing sun the tiny knives that are barely visible beat
against my ears
The sound of knocking on the eardrums doesn't tear the
eardrums that are about to tear
The faraway beating sound comes from faraway, faraway like
an echo
Let me in, let me in, let me in the sound is so faint that it
pleads with its needle-like hands
As eyes open a flock of crows darts out from my ears their
beaks poke at my pupils

A Blood-Clot Clock

Inside my heart there is a clock
that tick-tocks nonstop without skipping a single lifetime
There is a clock that
eats blood and shits blood
and its red branches have
spread all over my body
like the winter ivy with bare stems
encircling the cement clock on top of the tower

I have never been able to
get your clock to chime and no one
has disturbed my blood-clot clock
Does such a wretched clock have any thoughts?
Who was it that taught me –
a hundred years is short and a day is long?

I once fainted from staring at the sundial
I once threw my body into the sea
holding onto my clock, but I couldn't make it stop
no matter what kind of trauma or love

Since each of our starting times is different
our clocks point to different times
In our house the three of us sit in a circle
and silently feed our clocks
None of us has taken off
a clock and put it on the dining table

Ah ah, I tell you that I love you
in your ear with all my strength
as loudly as I can so your clock can hear me
and get your clock to chime
Is it all true – me saying I love you

and you saying you love me
tick-tocking at three in the afternoon?
We have never gone inside our clocks
As the gust of wind blows outside my clock
the red stems of the winter ivy
shake whoosh whoosh inside me
and tears collect in my eyes
Can you stop the clock hands for a moment?
Can you carry the handless clock against your breast?
When I bring my ear to your heart
the blood-clot clock runs by itself pang pang
it chimes right on time

The Poet and the Glamour Girl Go on a Hike

Tonight the poet and the glamour girl decide to go on a hike. The
first part of the trail is flat. The poet is used to easy hikes, but
the trail gets rockier as she climbs up. She slips, slides. Behind
the poet, the glamour girl snorts, Ha you can't even handle such
a short climb. The poet gets more out of breath as she climbs up
higher. The breathing of the two is wildly out of sync. The poet
nags for a rest. The glamour girl is getting hot, so she briskly
takes off the navy blue sky. Then she asks, Are you cold? Are you
cold? and bites the poet's frozen ears. This mountain must have
no compassion, compassion, says the poet wanting to put down
her heart, which is about to burst, but the trail keeps getting
steeper, and the glamour girl who is more experienced urges on
the poet who is out of breath, Don't put down your heart yet!
If we go back down now it's worse than not having come up at
all. The two stop arguing and watch the wrinkled ridge run up
gasping – it must have burst open a spring. The two make nice
and drink the spring water. They drink some and spill some.
The water spreads. It freezes under their feet till the ground
becomes slippery. Now the poet is totally exhausted, Getting
to the summit is too much, a mountain can't be swallowed in a
single gulp, and the rhythm of my breathing and walking is out

of sync, so this can't become a poem. But the glamour girl who
has been memorizing all the shapes of the valleys says, Why give
up now when the view is so fantastic? Then she unties the sun's
belt unrolling it. The sunset gets released at the corner of the sky
and the three temples with ThreeThousandBuddhaEnshrinement
CommemorationAllNightThreeThousandBowsDevotionalPrayer
written on them suddenly float up inside the poet's panting.
Tinkle tinkle – the sound of the landscape, as the poet embraces
the glamour girl and cries her eyes out. We have reached the lit
temples, the poet is moved, moved. Regardless, the glamour girl
closes her eyes and lets her hands relax and says, There's still the
ThreeThousandBows to do, and bites into the poet's neck.

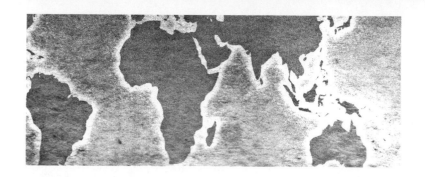

Al-Saddiq Al-Raddi
Seven poems
Translated from the Arabic by Sarah Maguire and Atef Alshaer

Al-Saddiq Al-Raddi is one of the leading African poets writing in Arabic today. He has gained a wide audience in his native Sudan for his imaginative approach to poetry and for the delicacy and emotional frankness of his lyrics. Saddiq was born in 1969 and grew up in Omdurman where he still lives. He is the cultural editor of *Al-Sudani* newspaper.

His first poetry collection *Songs of Solitude* was published in 1996 (second edition, 1999). He has also published *The Sultan's Labyrinth* (1996) and *The Far Reaches of the Screen . . .* (1999 & 2000); all three collections were published in one volume as Saddiq's collected poems in Cairo in 2009.

Saddiq came to the UK for the first time in 2005 to take part in The Poetry Translation Centre's World Poets' Tour, receiving a rapturous response from audiences here, both English-speaking and Sudanese. Since then he has returned to the UK to work with the PTC in 2006, 2008 and 2010. He took part in Poetry International in Rotterdam in 2010 and will be reading at the Berlin Poetry Festival in June 2012, as well as representing Sudan for Poetry Parnassus.

The Poetry Translation Centre published a dual-language chapbook of his work, *Poems*, in 2008; twenty-nine of his poems, in the original Arabic and in translation, are available on the PTC website, together with two podcasts of him reading alongside his translator, Sarah Maguire.

Longing

He knows how to light up his evenings
and brighten his mornings:
once, he would ignite her with sweat,
once, he would burnish her with song

Flushed,
he graces his cigarettes with an ode
He enflames a woman,
a mirror,
and a night –
as he rises through his cloud of smoke

Burnt,
he finds songs in the barrel of time
. . . . he snuffs out time.... and moves on
He longs for travel and freedom
Borne by the wind
. . . . . . he journeys
to his distant star

Throne

Aloft
as though lifted on fingertips –
and yet waves have no fingers
Her desire
structures the water –
and yet waves have no structure

In the split second
between crest and collapse
the world is created
and the world is annulled
without end

Record

King of the distant cries
Companion of screaming and silence –
Who saw you?

Who saw the blood on your roads?
Who prepared the watch and the spectacle of fear?
Who built the walls and threw a guard around them?
Who made the world die in the space of a word?

Memories of cities – fall
Expectations – fall
Histories of forgery – fall

Nothing

Before you start reading,
put down your pen:
consider the ink,
how it comprehends bleeding

Learn
from the distant horizon
and from narrowing eyes
the expansiveness of vision
and the treachery of hands

Do not blame me – do not blame anyone –
if you die before you read on
before blood is understood

Sympathy

I wince
whenever your name comes up
All ears, I seal my lips
keeping your secret a secret

(. . . Your mouth is ripe with desire
your eyes brim with tenderness
your body trembles as it calls. . .)

Anyone who mentions you cuts me to the quick,
and so I come to you in the heat of the noon
to whisper the story of dawn

You . . .
You . . .
My only creed!

A Body

The body of a bird in your mouth
breathing songs.
Raw light spills from your eyes,
utterly naked.

You must breach the horizon, once,
in order to wake up.
You must open window after window.
You must support the walls.

I let alphabets cling to me
as I climb the thread of language
between myself and the world.
I muster crowds in my mouth:
suspended between language and the world,
between the world and the alphabets.

I let my head
listen to the myth,
to all sides praising each other.
And I shout at the winds from the top of a mountain.

Why does my tongue tell me to climb this far?
What is the distance between my voice and my longing?
What is there?

A body transcending my body.
A body exiled by desire.
A body sheltered by the wind.

Some of Them Live with You

Some of them meet you
in the dark corners of the world
Some remain hidden

Some harbour revenge
or plot their escape
as they gallop down the valley of the wind

Some linger at the foot of a mountain
exposed to the elements

Some owned your heart
Some slaughtered it
Some stripped you naked

Some: me and you

Maya Sarishvili
Five poems
Translated from the Georgian by
Timothy Kercher and Nene Giorgadze

In 2008, Maya Sarishvili won the SABA Prize for Poetry, Georgia's top literature award, for her collection, *Microscope*. She is the author of one other poetry collection, *Covering Reality* (2001), as well as three radio plays. She lives in Tbilisi, Georgia where she works as a third-grade teacher and is mother to four children, ages 6 to 13. Her work is forthcoming or has appeared in *Guernica, Versal, Nashville Review, Los Angeles Review, Bitter Oleander,* and others. Georgian poet Zviad Ratiani explains her poetry best: 'Her poems are like Rilke's *Duino Elegies*: somehow self-sufficient, and somehow something is always happening inside them. Whenever I touch them, when I read them over and over again, something else is happening inside me each time. Her poems are naked, containing so much naked feeling and sense, but on the other hand, so much intelligence.'

To my father

I know what makes you scream in your sleep –
snakes rising from the candelabras
light up the room with their tongues.
And how frightening is that droning darkness,
poisoned with a treacherous light . . .
I know how every night you lather your own heart
like soap on your whole body.
How eager to remove the stains
with your own heart's foam.
Perhaps for that very reason
mother rises up from death every night
to plant roses in your slippers,
where you will move your feet in the morning . . .
Please find the sound of my childhood in our house.
It will probably be somewhere close to a box of sweets.
And if the little marmalade dog barks,
or anything like this,
then the curse has been broken . . .

To the neighbour

Look, the cold heating pipes
rise from your ceiling to our floor
and then go down again.
Our apartments are threaded on those bones,
in which there is death and nothing more.
They have stitched us together
floor by floor with this iron corpse

so that we won't escape
from a shared despair . . .
You told me how my mother was dying,
how she screamed: 'Help me, I beg you.'
And since then
that endless sentence is my bookmark –
always reminding me where I am,
where I stop . . .

How convincing peace is . . .

How convincing peace is
when fenced in by household things.
Daydreams so near the ground
they can't leap over the TV and lower cabinets.
How cleverly I fenced in
my decent life,
where nobody sees
how the seconds are a slap in the face –
right cheek, left cheek,
swiftly.
Sounds are flung from my mouth
and, like a shuttlecock, fly here and there,
falling apart, missing their marks . . .

This ice-cutter silence . . .

This ice-cutter silence
will slice through everything.
Where is the road that is coming for you?
Only the moon will be left like a kite.
I'll follow the line of its string
where there is an easing into losing patience
and an incurable silence
as if the blood lacks a sunset.
Below, a new day will start –
slide into my bed like a black spade into early morning soil –
digging me out from the dreams
that turned me over.

To Anastasia

She's impatient –
better she not look up –
double bent, the witch stories
spin like black-fire wheels
on the maternity ward ceiling.
But below there's such celebration –
red peonies fall from my body
and carry you out.
Although I am sprawled on the embroidered frame
and they make me scream,
I won't give away the secret
the drip hammers into my veins . . .

Évelyne Trouillot
'Tanpri'
Translated from the Creole by the author and from the French by Lynn Selby

Born in Port-au-Prince, Haïti, Évelyne Trouillot lives and works there as a French professor at the State Universtiy. She published her first book of short stories in 1996. In 2004, Évelyne Trouillot received the award: Prix de la romancière francophone du Club Soroptimist de Grenoble for her first novel *Rosalie l'infâme*. In 2005, her first piece for the theatre *Le bleu de l'île* received the Beaumarchais award from ETC Caraïbes.

Évelyne Trouillot has published two books of poetry: *Sans parapluie de retour* in 2001, and *Plidetwal* (in Creole) in 2005. Her poetry has been translated into Spanish and English and published in numerous issues of such magazines as *Bacchanales* of the Maison de la poésie of Rhône-Alpes in France; also in many anthologies, among them *Terre de femmes – 150 ans de poésie féminine en Haïti* (Éditions Bruno Doucey, France), and also in Canada, Mexico and Cuba .

Her latest novel *La mémoire aux abois*, published in France (Éditions Hoëbeke), in May 2010, received the Le prix Carbet de la Caraïbe et du Tout-Monde.

Tanpri

Tanpri
pa mande m pale de tranblendtè
Chak grenn blòk
ap rakonte m yon malè k poko fini
mwen pa rekonèt pwezi
kap sot nan bouch mwen
pawòl la chaje ak debri lanmò
ak retay lapenn
yo kole nan pwent dwèt mwen
yo pa vle kite m
tankou yon ekip lwa ki monte m
yo derefize ale
Pa pale m de 12 janvye
depi jou sa a
mwen tounen yon chwal yo monte
depi jou sa
m ap sèvi san m pa vle

septanm 2010

S'il te plaît (version française de l'auteur)

S'il te plaît
Ne me demande pas de te parler
Du tremblement de terre
Chaque amas de pierre
Me raconte un malheur en cours
Je ne reconnais pas la poésie
Qui coule de mes lèvres
Ce sont des mots
Débris de morts
Bris de détresses
Ils me collent aux doigts
Ils refusent de partir
Comme une horde d'esprits
Envahisseurs
Ils s'accrochent à moi
Ne me parle pas du 12 janvier
Depuis ce jour
Je suis chevauchée
Depuis ce jour
Je sers les esprits
Sans le vouloir

Please

Please
don't ask me to speak of
the earthquake
each single brick
keeps telling me of a misfortune with
no end
I don't recognize the poetry
coming out of my mouth
the words are burdened with the refuse of death
and remnants of grief
they stick to the tips of my fingers
they don't want to leave me
like a band of spirits that has taken over me
they refuse to go
Don't speak to me of January 12th
since that day
I've become a horse that they have
mounted
since that day
I serve them against my will

Translated by Lynn Selby

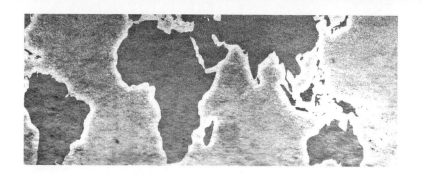

Mbarka Mint al-Barra'
'Poetry and I'
Translated from the Arabic by Joel Mitchell and The Poetry Translation Centre Workshop

Mbarka Mint al-Barra' is a Mauritanian poet and teacher who writes primarily in Arabic. A prominent figure in the cultural and literary life of her country, she has achieved some renown elsewhere in the Arab world, frequently attending literary festivals in other Arab countries.

Al-Barra' was born in al-Madhardhara, Mauritania, in 1957. In the country of the million poets, as Mauritania is often called, al-Barra' belongs to the third generation of modern poets. Like many of this group, she often uses dialogue and narrative in her poems as a means of addressing the realities of her society, borrowing images from religious texts, ancient Arab history and classical Arabic texts to portray conditions in Mauritania, the symbolism of religious stories being particularly effective in a country deeply rooted in Arab-Islamic traditions.

Al-Barra' has published works on both the social issues facing her country and its literature. Her collection of poetry, *Taranim li-Watanin Wahid* (Songs for a Country for All) was published in 1992. She has carried out extensive research into Mauritanian oral poetry, specifically the *tibra'*, a form of amorous poetry recited in

closed, women-only gatherings, and has translated *tibra'* poems
into French. A critical study, *Al-Shi'r al-Muritani al-Hadith, min
1970 ila 1995* (Modern Mauritanian Poetry, 1970–1995), was
published in 1998.

Note: The Poetry Translation Centre Workshop meets fortnightly in central
London and is open to anyone who can contribute translations of work by a
living poet from Africa, Asia or Latin America. To date, workshop members
have translated more than 100 poems, which can be read on the PTC website:
www.poetrytranslation.org

Poetry and I

The sin is that I wasn't a stone
   And the troubles of the world make me sleepless
And I shield myself with poetry
   And it keeps me company when I'm far from home
And poetry is my satchel that I will always carry with me
   It holds the taste and fragrance of the earth
It holds thickets of prickly branches
   It holds palm fronds loaded with dates
It paints all the stories of love in my language
   Its colours form the spectrum from grape to dawn
And I said bring the most beautiful of stringed instruments
   So the universe may know how music flows
And play its soothing melody
   That brings justice to those who are in love
Letters burden this world of mine
   Trouble leeches ink from the quill
Trouble leeches ink from the quill
   When I read of the longing of lovers I burn

Gerður Kristný
Thirteen poems
Translated from the Icelandic by Sigurður A. Magnússon and Victoria Cribb

---

Gerður Kristný was born on June 10, 1970 and brought up in Reykjavík. She graduated in French and comparative literature from the University of Iceland in 1992. She is a full- time writer. She won the Icelandic Literature Awards 2010 for her book of poetry *Blóðhófnir* which is based on an ancient Nordic myth, told in the Eddic poem Skírnimál, about the attempt of the Nordic fertility god Freyr to fetch the poet's namesake Gerdur Gymisdóttir from her far-away home as his bride. *Blóðhófnir* was also nominated for the Nordic Council Literature Prize. She is one of the most prolific contemporary writers in Icelandic. She has published collections of poetry and short stories, novels, books for children and a biography, for which she received The Icelandic Journalism Award in 2005. Her play, *The Dancing at Bessastadir*, based on two of her children's books, premiered in the Icelandic National Theatre in Reykjavík in February 2011 and was acclaimed by the public and critics alike. Other awards for her work include The Icelandic Children's Choice Award in 2003, The Halldór Laxness Literary Award in 2004 and The West-Nordic Children's Literature Award in 2010. She lives in

Reykjavík but travels regularly around the world to present her
work, giving readings in, among other places, Kampala, Cox's
Bazar, Maastricht and Colgata.

My brother and sister

Can't remember myself
without them

didn't really come into being
before they were born
with messages from the Almighty
inlaid in their soles

Haven't been able to decipher them
until now

the reason probably being
that I always walked ahead of them
thus never seeing their footprints

Request to be allowed
to keep the head start
beyond the grave

so that I will never remember myself
without them

(*Trs Sigurður A. Magnússon*)

Summer poem

In midsummer
the way between our homes
is blocked

the streets snowed up
and neither of us
wants to be the first
to clear away the snow

I remember that you were
not too keen on toil

and I have always
been fond of
snow

(*Trs Sigurður A. Magnússon*)

Prayer

Recall you still
before going to bed

sometimes
I say a prayer
that only includes you
and dreams about a tiny boat

Recall you also
when whetting the knife

know that the shortest way
to a man's heart
goes straight through
his chest

(*Trs Sigurður A. Magnússon*)

December

So this is the life
to which all other lives led

the morning black with darkness
murkier than the one
in which I fell asleep

your rod and your staff
raised for a blow

the whistling above my head
from the first moment

Then it is good to have a duvet
and even more so an embrace

(*Trs Sigurður A. Magnússon*)

God

When I die
you should carve
out of my teeth
biting frost

fashion whistles
out my bones
and play on them howls in the wind

Until then you will keep yourself remembered
by spreading lustre
on the freshly fallen snow

Above me hovers
your protective wing
not having shed
a single feather

(*Trs Sigurður A. Magnússon*)

New Year's Morning

The only ones to have
survived the night
are a Japanese family
who have switched off
the neon signs in their heads
and made do with the light
over the mountains

When the boy breaks the ice-film
on the lake with his toe
a low crack sounds
like the snap of a wing

He catches up with his parents
on the bridge where they
quicken their pace
They mean to be safe
indoors before
darkness reimposes
its curfew

(*Trs Victoria Cribb*)

Night

As you fall asleep
your arms slide apart
no shelter there for me now
the hatches burst
and the sea breaks through

I sink
through a thousand fathoms
not one of which
enfathoms me

Slowly the seabed
subsides
beneath the weight of my sleep

Foreboding heads my way
soon it will glide
into my dream

like a visitation

(Trs Victoria Cribb)

Departure

At the end
of the ramp
I inadvertently glance back

but you have vanished from view

Beyond the glass
a new day lifts itself
off the pavement
the blue of the mountains
spreads across my mind

as I turn
to continue on my way
I trip on my hem
my journey's designed
for a bigger woman than me

The plane waits on the runway
and I feel as if
the propeller's bitter blades
have entered my heart

(Trs Victoria Cribb)

Troy

Battlements rise against
the blind sky
The gods have turned
their backs on me
they incite against me
a mighty army
a frenzied throng
of darkness

Skin stretched over
the heel's hot blood

I whet my weapon
on the bones of my foes
then hack off the heel

Draw my knife as the sun sets
sleep now, I'll hew you a horse

(*Trs Victoria Cribb*)

Ægisiða

Oyster catcher scurrying
over the sand
made by the master's hand
– like you

And now it's said
you've gone
to a better place

I doubt that
for there was nothing wrong
with this one till now
when the grasses huddle
fearfully on the bank

– a thousand fingers invoking God

(*Trs Victoria Cribb*)

Langanes

We sat in the black bay
open sea to the east
homefield flecked with sheep
sky with high-flying wings

Then came the fog
veiling mountain, sky and dog
You went before me
into the vanished house

I should probably
have knelt in prayer
given thanks for this day
but who was I
to interrupt God

the many-voiced whisper
of the moor?

(*Trs Victoria Cribb*)

Triumph

The farmer drives gloating
through the district
vixen dead on the hood

He laid siege to her lair
in his jeep
so the animal smelt
the stench of petrol
not man

No one mentions
Achilles or Hector
and I know how to
hold my tongue

(*Trs Victoria Cribb*)

Skagafjörður

I try to be
kind to the children
so they'll tend my grave
when the time comes
crumble biscuits in the grass
on my birthday
and recite the poem about
the gambolling cows
themselves grown old and grey

All the same I will
know them again
by the heavenly smell of the stable

may they always be fragrant as the Jesus child

(Trs Victoria Cribb)

Anise Koltz
Four poems
Translated from the French by
Anne-Marie Glasheen

Anise Koltz, born in Luxembourg in 1928, first wrote in German. After the death of her husband, a late victim of the Nazi occupation, she found she could no longer do so. After a long period of silence, she began to write again, but almost exclusively in French. She has also written children's books in Luxembourgish.

A poet of international renown, Koltz actively promotes the literature of Luxembourg. She founded and, from 1963 to 1974, directed the *Journées littéraires de Mondorf* which brought together writers from all over the world, with the aim of establishing and maintaining links between the Luxembourg and the international literary scene. In 1995, the Mondorf Literary Days were revived and represented all genres, thereby providing a wide range of authors with a platform for their works.

Koltz is a member of the Académie Mallarmé (Paris), Pen-Club Belgium, and Institut Grand-Ducal des Arts et des Lettres (Luxembourg). She is one of the founding members of The European Academy of Poetry. Over the years she has collaborated with poets, writers and artists to create bibliophilic editions, had a variety of works dedicated to her, and had poems set to music. She continues to be honoured with prestigious awards. Translations of her poetry have appeared in Belgium, Colombia, Germany, Ireland, Italy, Macedonia, Portugal, Rumania, Spain and Sweden. In the UK, *At the Edge of Night* (a collection of poems from four of her books and translated by Anne-Marie Glasheen) was published by ARC Visible Poets in 2009.

Do not come back Ulysses . . .

Do not come back Ulysses –

I'm wary of the mad dog
who guards your heart

I'm afraid of your nets
in which I wrestle
of your name that makes my mouth bleed

Disappear with the sun
behind the hills

Do not come back Ulysses

Rise up and Walk

To the memory of René Koltz

I speak of the beloved
He is everywhere
With no way out his feet
plead a new destiny

When I lower my lids
see him walk
through town
held by my gaze

The slightest flutter
of my lashes
trips him
and kills him again
before my very eyes

I have gathered
the still warm and trembling
pieces of him

There where nothing is lost
nothing is created
I want to bring him back to life

Do not save me
one day
like him
I shall return

In the meantime
I shall sink
into the earth
toward his skeleton

I shall resemble him
he will recognise me

My shadow

Attached for life
to my shadow
which collapses to the ground
I grow dizzy
stumbling
over the pool of black blood
over this mirage of myself

On your suitcase

Tomorrow my love
we shall sleep
entwined on your suitcase

Into which I put my moans
the tears
I can no longer shed

When you leave
the hairs of your beard will fall
one by one

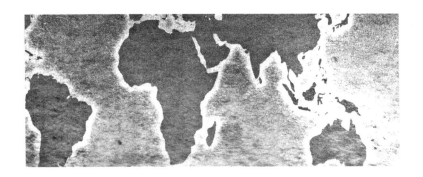

Soleïman Adel Guémar
'Eyes closed'
Translated from the French by Tom Cheesman and John Goodby

Soleïman Adel Guémar is about the same age as the independent republic of Algeria. He worked there as a freelance journalist, investigating human rights violations and corruption, until 2002, when he claimed political asylum in the UK following threats to his life connected with his efforts to found an independent publishing house. He now lives in south Wales. 'Eyes closed' belongs to a slowly growing body of work written in exile. Poems he wrote in Algeria, originally published in diverse newspapers and magazines there and in France, are collected in *State of Emergency* (Arc Publications: Visible Poets series, 2007) – French originals with English verse translations by Tom Cheesman and John Goodby. The book won an English PEN Writers in Translation award. As Lisa Appignanesi remarked in her introduction: 'Britain has inadvertently inherited a political poet of stature, one whose language sings . . .'. A volume of Adel Guémar's prose – stories, satires and parables from Algeria, translated by Tom Cheesman – has just been published by Hafan Books in Swansea under the title *Local Therapy* (see: lulu.com/hafan).

Eyes closed

1

And so at last I left
Wounded from head to foot
Dreams all fuddled
But still intact I tell myself intact
Revived by the brilliantly nubile showers

I took my time in the early morning
Sipping a mint tea in the local café
Before catching a flight to the far side of the world
Three hours away from the cemetery-republic
Where I'd spent my life waiting for a miracle

I cast a last glance back
At the electrically-operated gates
Of the new masters' plush residences
Thrown up in haste
As if to guard against the evil eye
And any chance of ghosts of justice waking

2

Odours of the terroir that keep breaking in
Bring back the vertigo of being dangled
From the topmost floor over a city
Deformed but so beautiful still
Over the heads that throng the streets
Lit by the torches of sham celebrations
Over a sea embellished
With small boats all adrift
Over the bars packed with hardened informers
And nightclubs run by colonel torturers

Over the ceaseless aftershocks of an earthquake censored
Hunted down into the narrowest fissures
Of the tectonic plates of my surviving memory
Of the time of dry heaves flooded in blood

3

I swigged out of dubious bottles
I smoked everything forbidden

It's so quiet I'm hearing
The voices of my childhood
Singing in chorus

I sat myself down on the ground
I wiped clean the white marble of the spat-upon tomb
And I fell asleep

4

Your hand seeks me in the night
Timidly it wakes me
And halts at my heart
Lingering there
Clutch and caress both

Your hair it covers my face
I inhale perfume of the ocean
The henna'd Sahara of your passions
The breath of trees of virgin forests
In the spring when they're for being lost in

On your back I trace those flowers
I've yet to give you
And your tender insurrectionary eyes
You've bewitched me with

I broke my watch
Attempting in vain to stop time

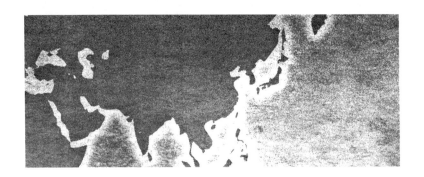

Hadaa Sendoo
Five Poems
Translated from the Mongolian by Richard Berengarten and the author

---

Hadaa Sendoo was born in Inner Mongolia in 1961. Since 1991 he has lived and worked in Ulaanbaatar. He writes in Mongolian, Chinese and English. He has published more than ten collections of poetry. His poems have been translated into more than thirty languages (English: *Come Back to Earth,* 2009). His work has been selected for *The Best Mongolian Poetry*. He won the Mongolian Writers Union Prize. Hadaa Sendoo was elected a full Member of the Mongolian Academy of Humanities and has received an Achievement Award (2010, USA). Hadaa Sendoo's most recent publication in Mongolian is *The Road Is Not Completed*, published in Ulaanbaatar, 2011. He has been nominated for the 2012 International Peace Award. He is also a founder and leading figure of the *World Poetry Almanac*.

A red moon and my father

One night
my father's face
flickered in the dark

In his hand
a fire-red cigarette end
like a red moon, slow-moving

Cuckoo song

Sunset glow
swaying back and forth
on reeds

Cuckoo – cuckoo – cuckoo

Memory of love burning
in and through my cheeks
a tender kiss

Cuckoo – cuckoo – cuckoo

When I last heard you
it was like the very first time
in my golden hometown

Gobi

When I reach the Gobi –
be calm and clear, my mind –
gallop, wild asses and gazelles –
stone, become a mirror –
whatever time was, be forgotten –
whatever troubles are, disappear –

And when I go back to the city of death –
With that wind still flowing in my hands –
I miss the Gobi Desert:
a Mongolian rat peeping out of his hole –
a red camel –
and a Gobi girl –
tanned by the sun –

Fog

often appears in the morning
between rolling hills
a hazy wonderland –

an apparently calm face
which may be an illusion
perhaps a vast trap

Fire

You're the highland's ancient song
eagle dance, shaman's drum –

you're thinking, soul
pain –

you're the meaning of woods burning
nomads –

horses passing through night
blue rapids

Razmik Davoyan
Five poems
Translated from the Armenian by
Armine Tamrazian

Razmik Davoyan is Armenia's most prominent living writer, with seventeen collections of poetry, three children's books, three prose works and one novel published in his own country, and with translations of his work published throughout the world. Born in 1940, he studied Philology and History at university, and worked as an editor for a literary magazine, before being appointed to a series of government posts, including Advisor to the President of the Republic of Armenia. Razmik Davoyan has received numerous literary awards, including, in 1986, Armenia's State Prize for Literature, in 1997, the Order of St. Mesrop Mashtots, in 2003, the President's Prize for Literature, in 2010, First Degree Medal For Services to the Motherland. In English he was published by Arc in their 'Visible Poets', no. 27 (2010).

I called upon the touch of fingers . . .

I called upon the touch of fingers –
                        It wasn't there.
I looked at my image in glass lips –
I squeezed the tulip
And its black sorrow
Remained in my hands.

Somewhere, a birch wood is being stolen now . . .

Somewhere, a birch wood is being stolen now,
Somewhere, skies are stolen,
Somewhere, a dream . . .
Somewhere, they are stealing eternally
And the light cowers
In the yellow arms of the lamps.

Torn balloons scattered in the dust . . .

Torn balloons scattered in the dust
The city was inflated with joy yesterday,
Feverish with celebrations, it was twirling in the air,
In people's eyes.
The balloons burst from joy, yesterday –
Today, a bare, dusty
Torn silence,
Drags itself along
In the streets
Together with exhausted feet,
On the cobblestones,
In my brain.

My voice glides through your wet streets . . .

My voice glides through your wet streets,
It disappears among the roses
Which climb over your rooftops.
Through your soft evening
Dreams pass by with the reflections of shining billboards.
And I hug myself with your arms
To keep the dust in your corners
From stirring with the autumn leaves.

We speak of the miracles of life

(From 'Requiem')

We are bored with life
But when gathering
We speak of the miracles of life.

With the wingless dreams
Of the nights
Spread over the emptiness,
Climbing to the peaks of emptiness
And from the deepest gorges of this life,
Having placed our hearts
Between our inviting lips
Like Havana cigars,
We were speaking of the miracles of life.
In the opening of each other's eyes
With the harmonious music of the hand,
In the blue-red mists of the heart
And between stiff lips
We watch our daily life.
'The Earth is born each day,
The Earth grows
It multiplies like thoughts . . .'
We speak of the miracles of life.

In our dark brains
With the sparkle of vague unearthly nights
Fever gropes about
And human sin jingles in the jet black ears of darkness.

We are humbled
Before our sins as a dark night
Before the sun . . .
Oh, pitiful night
You couldn't thicken your darkness enough
To flash a white ray of light,
A mere ray of white light with which
You could have filled millions of eyes
And covered the encaged sorrow
Of millions of souls.
You could have stood as the main pillar
In millions of thoughts
And axis the universe.

Yet –
Kissing the wet lips of your darkness
I embrace you –
With your infinite, endless darkness
You cannot fill a single eye,
The pupil of one soul –
Be the ending of the average song,
A sanctuary for the average god,
A criminal for the average craze
A masculine voice for the average whore,
Conventional femininity
For the average woman,
You cannot be
The tragic or happy ending
For the average life,
Its future
For you are so non-average.

We are bored with life
But we speak of the miracles of life

*

My relations are lining up beside me now
Each a swimmer of eternity,
There is a melting stiffness on their faces
Which time makes its own
Before my very eyes.
Taking it, absorbing it,
Sticking it to itself now.
Time brings them to me
Their unexpected appearance
Sprinkles perfume upon my quivering lips.
Relations, sombre relations,
Where are you disappearing to, evaporating alive . . .
They fly away from my hands like birds.
From their silent eyes
Like immaterial, endless ribbons of yearning
I pull
All the streets of the world
And spread them over the earth
And leaving a trail of dusty footprints behind
I walk over the asphalt of melted black eyes.
Glorified cities
And big
And rich with past history
And romantic with today's life
As a thousand-legged spider
On a white wall
As a white hand moving in the dark
Or as myself
  On the peak of Mount Ararat,
  At the beginning of time,
  On a boat,
  Alone,
  Saved from the flood.
I pull our cities from their eyes
And in their place there remains
The nocturnal blue silence of the old city,
And in the silence,
As the voice of a poet reading his poems

In the monk's cell,
There remains sorrow
Melted in the stones of forgotten cobbled streets,
There remains the blinding, unborn fog
Buried in seas living in forgetfulness,
The black raincoats, hanging from pegs on the walls . . .
There remains –
                        A bare world, Earth
Made of feelings,
And on faces
Two points of darkness framed in light
Woven from yearnings.

The raincoats wear us
For them true rain still exists,
Truer than these white walls,
The humble pegs
And us.

And we,
Bearing lightning rods upon our shoulders
For heads,
Emerge to tie
All the unconnected streets together
To make one whole wide world
With sphinxes sitting on eyelashes,
With the Mass of female bodies
Lying in the transparent shadow of eyelids,
With the untameable life of rhythms
Squeezed in the hands,
In our bodies
With the tiny, opened eyes
And the opened lips of millions of innocent children
Living in our eyes,
Fearless of light...
We speak of
        The miracles
        Of life.

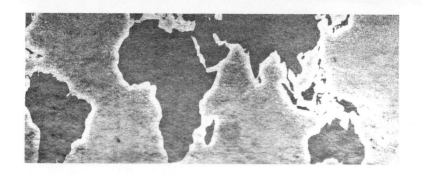

Abdullahi Botan
Three poems
Translated from the Somali by Rob Inglis

Abdullahi Botan is a Somali poet who has earned his living in London doing any job he could get and learning English as he went along.

The word 'sir' in English sounds identical to the Somali word for 'secret'. When Abdullahi Botan received his first official letter, and he knew the first word had the sound 'sir', he carried it around in his pocket for two days, occasionally glancing down at it furtively, till, in a place where he could not be observed, he asked a friend to translate it for him.

Officialese

If a letter begins with 'Unfortunately'
Then be certain it won't contain anything good
In fact, if the first phrase is not 'I am pleased'
You are doomed.

Hoppa

Hoppa – you will triumph!
Your destiny unfurls!

Hoppa – what loads you have carried!
I couldn't have managed alone,
sharing the bitter grey morning
through wind, hail, sleet and rain
from Somers Town to King's Cross
and the Cromer Street Café.

As camels bring food in Somalia,
for three long years you've provisioned
the Cromer Street Café clientele.
I load you until you're overflowing,
seize your handle, and call: 'Hooha'
and you, never lazy or sluggish,
rise like an eagle flapping its wings,
your wheels pad like the great bird's feet
as it strives for speed to fly,
or the whirring tyres of an airliner
tilting its nose towards the sky.

You're like the camel we call Hayin,
we trust it to carry the old folks and children,
its nature is honest, its spirit is willing
it carries a load without breakage or spilling.

Hoppa – you will triumph!
Your destiny unfurls!

What a cornucopia you deliver:
– coffee and meat and pancakes and pasta,
all the way from my flat where they're prepared –
to the waiting, ravenous café customers,
who smile as your presence informs them:
'See what riches I have brought you.
Say goodbye to all your hunger!'

There is no way I would exchange you
for Honda, Hyena, or Toyota.
You never pollute, no route defeats you,
no street is too narrow, no corner too sharp,
no hill too steep, no bus too hard to board,
you have no fear of parking tickets
and ignore congestion charges.
Could Boris hitch you to his bike
to execute an opening lap,
thus giving our Olympic Games
a smart distinction from Beijing?

As oil becomes a trickle
and vain expansion slows,
you are the role model needed
by our throwaway society.
You hover on the starting blocks,
your wheels and axles oiled.

Hoppa – you will triumph!
Your destiny unfurls!

Note: 'Hoppa' is the shopping trolley vital to the poet as proprietor of
the Cromer Café.

Mirror Image

A youth might say that come what may
he'll never desert the land of his birth.
But one day a problem comes his way
and he has to run without his shirt.
What's his answer, do you suppose,
when he's asked to show his passport?

If someone's lost in the dead of night
he can find his way in the next day's light.
You can call him lucky – you case is worse
if you've had to run without your shirt
and even the light of the following day
might never help you find your way.

A Somali who is a refugee
describes his condition as *isdhiip* – 'surrender'
even when he's escaped to a distant land
where he's accepted and is free.
That word *isdhiip* used repeatedly
eats its way into his brain.

Hold a mirror up to that word *isdhiip*
– in reverse it becomes *biidhsi* –
and *biidhsi* means to earn something,
to think clearly and be positive,
and never to let the thought of 'surrender'
enter your brain when awake or sleeping.

Kristiina Ehin
Three poems
Translated by Ilmar Lehtpere

Kristiina Ehin is one of the leading poets in Estonia. Most of her work, poetry and prose, has also appeared in English translation, including the Poetry Society Popescu Prize winner *The Drums of Silence* (Oleander Press, 2007), the Poetry Book Society Recommended Translation *The Scent of Your Shadow* (Arc, 2010) and *The Final Going of Snow* (*MPT* Poets, 2011). An as yet untitled volume of her new and selected poems in English translation will be published this year in the US by the Bitter Oleander Press. She has been chosen by the Southbank Centre to represent Estonia at the Poetry Parnassus Festival. Her English translator is Ilmar Lehtpere.

At the fire's edge . . .

At the fire's edge
everything has a scent, moves and hums
and when I stretch my toes out
the forest begins
Like a dark green blanket
it spreads out over the land
and reaches
you as well
and over you
and the very same fire
reaches you too
and the very same June
and St John's

You are there somewhere
a crown of fern blossoms on your head
boots and heart muddy
beard shaved
mobile shining and clean
and full of women's phone numbers
the same summer in your eyes
the same June and St John's

Totally unsuitable for being a man
but completely Pan

However we tried . . .

However we tried
the shadows still touched
Paper-white swans flew over the lighthouse
We stood and watched
how the light faded

Here no one can see
when we walk hand in hand
There is only the sea and
the empty shore
There is a bone-white moon
in the blood-dark sky

and the past that has been unlocked
and keeps on flowing
over the dear warm kiss of the present

Children are building . . .

Children are building
a tower out of big blocks
in the ferry play area
Estonian and Russian children together

Zdes podhodit!
Put it here!

They laugh
when it falls over
They ooh and aah
as it gets higher

Hvatit uže!
No one more block!

A quarrel arises
Mothers hurry closer
One mother says
Mnogo že igrušek igraite vmeste!
Another mother admonishes
Be friendly!

The last block is placed

This ferry's tower of Babel
really did get finished
and languages didn't get in the way

Immanuel Mifsud
Two poems
Translated from the Maltese by
Maria Grech Ganado

Immanuel Mifsud (Malta, 1967) has published poetry, prose and also three children's books. His prose has been considered very controversial and critics have tagged him the leading writer of the Maltese Generation-X. Mifsud's writing career oscillates between having a short story collection banned in 2005 and being criticised by the media for his very graphic writing, and winning the National Literary Award in 2002 and the European Union Prize for Literature in 2011. Several of his prose works have been translated, most notably his short story collection *Happy Weekend* (in English and Albanian), his novella *Zerafa* (in English and German) and his European Award winning book *In the Name of the Father (and of the Son)* which has been translated and published in English with forthcoming editions in French, Slovene, Czech, Turkish and Bulgarian. Since Immanuel Mifsud is frequently invited to participate in poetry festivals various poems of his have been translated. In 2005 Maurice Riordan translated his poetry collection *Confidential Reports* (Cork, Southword Editions) and in 2011 *Bateau Noir* (Malta, Edizzjonijiet Emmadelezio) was published in a bilingual edition Maltese-French with translations by Nadia Mifsud.

Immanuel Mifsud lectures in Maltese modern poetry and literary theory at the University of Malta.

A poem before you sleep

Since, when I look at you, it's not you I see
I see a whole swarm of butterflies
flying together without a destination;
I see a long stretch of sand embrace the sea;
I see the wind which has finally begun to love me:
cities I visited and the streets I roamed:
the flowers waking one by one.
And now a long river full of the colour
of petals which have once more come to life.
Since when I look at you it's not you I see
I see every thing reborn in a new form.

Tell me: where are the butterflies fleeing to?
Which sandy beach, which sea will welcome them?
Which wind will embrace them so they can fly
towards cities gathered in streets both wide and narrow?
What flowers will they sip?

Because when I
cast my eyes upon you, it's not you I see.
I see a poem as wide as the horizon;
I see a poem I never dreamt of;
a poem hanging like a necklace
before my face gazing at you and wondering
at the speed with which you fly towards the sea
of roads without end or corners
where the blossoms of hope and waiting dwell.

Now let us turn the light off and go to sleep
Look, these are fresh sheets which have been laid.

Nina Czerkies

Nina Czerkies sings like a wounded bird.
Her hands too: as soon as they alight on her guitar
turn into wings dripping blood.
Or it might be the vodka scribbling pictures
I gathered at the corners of Warsaw
which have nothing in common with this night
in this apartment overflowing with the music
which only solitude can register.

Chen Li
'Dancers of Delphi'
Translated by Chang Fen-ling

Chen Li (陳黎, 1954–) was born in Hualien, Taiwan. Regarded as 'one of the most innovative and exciting poets writing in Chinese today', he is the author of eleven books of poetry and a prolific prose writer and translator. With his wife Chang Fen-ling, he has translated into Chinese the works of many poets, such as Heaney, Hughes, Plath, Neruda, Paz, and Szymborska, and has published over a dozen volumes of translations. He is the organizer of the annual Pacific Poetry Festival in his hometown. His poems have been translated into several languages. Among the volumes are *Intimate Letters: Selected Poems of Chen Li*, translated into English by Chang Fen-ling.

Dancers of Delphi

There wandering, a lad with his lute and poems.
There, under the moonlit laurel tree,
the dancers of Delphi sprinkled wine all over the ground
and the moon fell into a trance.
Those fond of asking riddles kept swinging their hair-trailing
    heads,
thinking of nothing but melancholy and dark thick eyebrows.
How did he know,
how would he suspect those whirling myrtles and ivies
    weren't their bodies?
How would he? Such exquisite and life-like description.
Smiles, sculptural reliefs, all the mysterious occurrences.
There, the dancers of Delphi sprinkled wine all over the
    ground.
There, a lad with his lute and poems.

Note: The title of this poem comes from a piano piece by Claude Debussy
(*Preludes*, book 1, no.1).

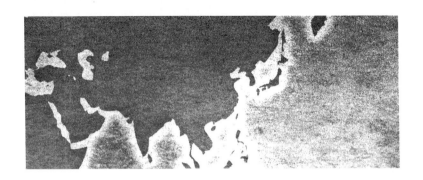

Yuyutsu RD Sharma
Five poems
Translated from the Nepali by the author

Yuyutsu RD Sharma is a distinguished poet and translator. He has published nine collections of poetry and, recently, a translation into Nepali of the Hebrew poet Ronny Someck. He has translated and edited several anthologies of contemporary Nepali poetry in English. His own work has been translated into German, French, Italian, Slovenian, Hebrew, Spanish and Dutch. He has just published *Annapurnas & Stains of Blood*, a work of non-fiction (Nirala, 2010), and completed his first novel. He is the founder of *Kathya Kayakalpa* (Content Metamorphosis), a new literary movement in Nepali poetry.

Born at Nakodar, Punjab and educated at Baring Union Christian College, Batala, and later at Rajasthan University, Jaipur, Yuyutsu remained active in the literary and theatrical circles of Rajasthan, appearing in plays by Shakespeare, Brecht, Pinter, and Albee, for example. Later he taught at various campuses of Punjab University and Tribhuwan University, Kathmandu.

The Library of Congress has nominated his recent book of Nepali translations entitled *Roaring Recitals; Five Nepali Poets* as 'Best Book of the Year 2001 from Asia' under the Program, 'A World of Books: International Perspectives'.

Currently, Yuyutsu edits *Pratik, A Magazine of Contemporary Writing* and writes a literary column for Nepal's leading daily, *The Himalayan Times*. Half the year, he travels all over the world to read from his works and to conduct creative-writing workshops at various universities in North America and Europe. Back home, he goes trekking in the Himalayas.

More: www.yuyutsu.de

Chorten, Muktinath

A castle of souls,
a song of sublime stones
in the timeless manuscript
of racing winds and rain shadows,
cotton puffs of clouds drunk
from rugged symmetry of brown rocks and Dhaulagiri peaks

You could pass by it,
gasping in the thin air,
a fledgling flame,
an angry oracle mourning over
the loss of fruit and fibre,
roots and blood-red geraniums' ripe reminiscences . . .

Or could stay a moment,
place a pagoda of your breath on its crusty rim
or an oval black stone
to the shrine of shining stars
to consummate an ample union
of moon and sun in broad daylight.

A crumbling jar,
a terracotta horoscope
of hope and history,
you could earn a quiet morsel
of compassion as God's blessed food
to be dropped into
your father's gaping mouth
that remained open
even after he passed away,
right after his return from
decade-long ramblings among Naga ascetics
in the forests of rain and rites
before he disappeared
without a trace
on the ladder of time, climbing
into the blue of the wailing skies . . .

First Visitors

'Green Paradise'
somewhere in the central Himalayas
that lured them in the fifties,
the first visitors who met up
in a bar or restaurant in Calcutta or Varanasi
and planned to wrangle permission
to enter the forbidden land,
the first clouds from the West
that came riding Indian Dakota airplane
to land in Gauchar,
the bullock-driven carts that came
to collect the luggage

as the precious passengers came down
the wooden ladders in a cow field,
and silence,
yes, silence watched,
a scared little mouse
in the long grassed field,
felt its tremors, the first sparks
that flew up in the sapphire skies
to explode the castle of cicada silences.
Bill Tilman, Boris Lissannivich, Maurice Herzog,
wind in their hair, fire in their fists,
hammering nails in crisp snow
of just found land, the bitch that
bit them in their dreams,
now stood up above, snivelling . . .
Can one ever return to the scene of silence?
Bells shaking their tongues
to wake the mating serpents
from a stupor of a million centuries,
the visiting breath harsh
on the rounded eyes of Naga natives,
ruthless footfalls breaking
the needle of time in the throats of punctual
roosters of green canyons . . .
Moon's shadow squinted,
Sun squirmed, dragons in the monasteries
of high cliffs stopped singing fire
out of their eternal throats and
the glaciers began to melt . . .

Lost in the Annapurnas
for Sukrity, Rachel and Alison

Lost a T-shirt
near a crystal waterfall

a notebook
with names of birds and shamans of the canyons

finches, larks and red-billed choughs
swifts, lammergeiers, griffins and redstarts

my rainbow-coloured umbrella
with flowers and a million butterflies trapped in it

one of the lenses
of my looking glass in a pond at Hot Springs

lost excess fat,
double chin, pouch of my belly,

drooling flesh of my cheekbones
lost worries of my city struggles

in the leech-greasy forests,
oak and maple, conifers and rhododendrons

threw a copy of the bestseller
over the rusty bars of a squeaking wooden ridge

for the bearded goats
of the famed valleys to read and rejoice

lost fears
of finding right words

perfect dreams,
faultless partners along

narrow cliffside tracts
skirting utter
horror of highest precipices

lost my unease
along with my troubled heart

to the glaciers
of Annapurnas . . .

Phurba's sight,
Ghangyul

Before entering
the Langtang forest

before Shermathang
before the flight of birds of heaven

rushing in the Breaking News
of more rain, thunder and snow

I caught a flash of her
in the last house of Ghangyul

a juniper tree
bent beneath the flutter of colourful flags

quietly collecting barley
and millet drying out in the spacious courtyards.

I walked past her,
humbled and hushed

and entered the forest
risking blizzards and snowstorms

the wise one who had known
the secret fragrance

of the forests
of the whole world.

Phurba's earrings

Phurba's earrings
of studded stars

glistening grains
of hail falling in sunlight

against the jet black
of her long tresses

by her cheekbones
of proverbial Helambu apples

Phurba's face
blaze of a midday sun

behind fluttering
prayer flags and crystalline waterfalls

Phurba's earrings
of five milk ponds

dug from
the shy earth's womb

by lord Shiva's
shaking trident,

Phurba's earrings . . .

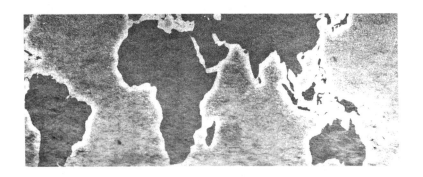

Bewketu Seyoum
Eight poems
Translated from the Amharic by the author
with Chris Beckett and Alemu Tebeje

Bewketu Seyoum is a popular young Ethiopian poet and writer. He grew up in Mankusa, a small town in Gojjam on the road to Lake Tana, source of the Blue Nile. He studied psychology and English at Addis Ababa University. His father is an English teacher and his mother comes from a family of Orthodox Christian priests. His first collection of Amharic poems, *Nwari Alba Gojowoch (Unmanned Houses)*, was published in 2002 and has since been reprinted three times. He has published two further collections of poetry, two best-selling novels and two CDs of short stories (some of which can be heard on YouTube).

Bewketu's poems are short and punchy, full of warmth, humour and humanity. Living in a country where freedom of speech and political dissent are very limited, where even to question religious practices can earn you a severe beating (as happened to Bewketu last year), his poems are rarely confessional. They read more like folk proverbs or traditional religious poems called *q'ene,* but they never lack personal commitment or courage. Bewketu also uses more rhyme and sound play in his poems than we have managed to translate, but then Amharic is a wonderfully playful and plosive language.

In 2008, Bewketu was awarded the prize for Best Young Writer of the year by the President of Ethiopia.

The door to freedom

When tortured spirits
who live their life in chains
are suddenly called to freedom,
when the door of their cell
is thrown open and the guards sent home,
they will not feel truly free
unless they break through the wall.

To the runner with a limping heart

To build up your legs, don't just butter your soup,
to sail over bumps, don't rely on your shoes –
    call the man who trains hearts!

Your feet do the running, but if your heart limps,
    you won't catch what you're after,
    you won't leave where you flee.

There is a man

Look! Diogenes the Dog is playing the fool:
'Where is an honest man?' he cries,
while swinging a man-made sun from his finger.

Decorating the universe

Instead of escaping into the woods of people
where my body could misbehave,
I hunted for poems
and I was prodigal with poetry.

But flies are more honest than poems
and while I decorate the universe,
they show me that my room is full of dust.

The one who falls and the one who lifts

I saw him lying on the ground,
so I knelt to help him stand.
But he was downcast,
his strength had turned to dust.
We had not fallen together,
so I could not be his brother.

The empty kettle

The night is roaring!
The fire is burning!
My busy-boy fingers
are scooping up sticks,
putting my empty kettle on the stove,
my kettle that cannot boil over –
just to share the absence of steam!

Tramp's country

Let my country be this tent,
the bundle I carry on my back:
a tent is easy to uproot
when they move me on,
and easy to pitch in the dark.

I won't climb a mountain

I won't climb a mountain
to touch the clouds,
I won't lift the frown
of a rainbow into a smile,
I won't borrow
Tekle Haymanot's wings
or Jacob's ladder –
when I want to climb,
skies will come down to me!

MPT Poetry Translation Competition

I suspect that in many poetry competitions the judges have to discard three quarters of the entries on the grounds of quality before they make a shortlist, whereas the remarkable thing about this competition, the first organized by *MPT*, was the high standard of the poems submitted. This made the choice all the more difficult. We could have found at least twenty of the seventy-one poems on the subject of freedom to be worthy winners of our modest prize money.

One exciting aspect of reading them was that you never knew if the next poem was coming from Burma, Russia or Bolivia, whether it would be a translation of Cavafy, Darwish or Joachim du Bellay. This was a truly international and encompassing project, which reflects the spirit of our Olympic issue; and the subject, freedom, proved a good choice for the translators. The range of countries and languages was vast. We received poems from Arabic, Burmese, Chinese, Estonian, French, Gaelic, German, Italian, Polish, Portuguese, Russian, Swedish, Welsh, Yiddish . . .

As we read, we were reminded of the many injustices and horrors in our history, from the death camps to the oppressions of contemporary regimes. We all know about these things but we constantly need to be reminded of them, and those translations, those poems, are the means of reminding us, as vividly as the television pictures now coming out of Syria. There was a poem written from the ghetto in 1940, for instance, and a poem about Theresienstadt. There was a poem about Aung Sun Suu Kyi as well as poems about being in prison in Russia and in the Middle East. But the subject of freedom gave rise to many different interpretations. There was an impressive translation of Victor Hugo's poem about Freedom in Education, which nicely contrasted with the translation of Prévert's joyful poem about the dunce, and Brecht's about slavery. But our contributors also found inspiration in poems which were not only cries against oppression, but celebrations of that vital element in any human life, and in any country or culture: individual freedom; so there were beautiful poems by Ehin in Estonia and Machado in Spain, and one from Poland by Agnieszka Wolny-Hamkało which perfectly caught the freedom and adventure of travelling, and which made it into our list of runners-up.

The seventy-one entries were by a total of fifty-one translators, since some submitted more than one entry. We had fifteen entries from previous contributors to the magazine, and thirty-six who had never before sent us any poems. There were one or two disqualifications because the submitted poems/translations were too long.

The three judges, David Constantine, Sasha Dugdale and myself, narrowed the field to ten poems each, making decisions initially on the quality of the poem, the translation of the 'spirit' of the original, the relevance to the subject, and the attention to form. Choices were compared, discussed many times, and the eventual winners' poems were checked for accuracy in translation by qualified linguists, a necessary step because, needless to say, the judges do not speak all the world's languages (although, through editing *MPT*, they know people who can!)

The winning poems are published here, along with a short explanation by the translators of how they went about translating their poems.

Helen Constantine

First prize

A translation by Ingar Palmlund of Tomas Tranströmer's
'Allegro'.

Allegro

I play Haydn after a dark day
and sense an honest warmth in my hands.

The keys are willing. Mild hammers strike.
The tone is green, lively and still.

The tone says that freedom exists
and that someone does not pay the emperor tribute.

I push the hands deep into my haydnpockets,
mimicking one who quietly watches the world.

I raise the haydnflag – this means:
'We do not surrender. But want peace.'

The music is a glasshouse on the slope
where stones fly, stones roll.

And the stones roll right through
but each pane remains whole.

Allegro

Jag spelar Haydn efter en svart dag
och känner en enkel värme i händerna.

Tangenterna vill. Milda hammare slår.
Klangen är grön, livlig och stilla.

Klangen säger att friheten finns
och att någon inte ger kejsaren skatt.

Jag kör ner händerna i mina haydnfickor
och härmar en som ser lugnt på världen.

Jag hissar haydnflaggan — det betyder:
"Vi ger oss inte. Men vill fred."

Musiken är ett glashus på sluttningen
där stenarna flyger, stenarna rullar.

ch stenarna rullar tvärs igenom
men varje ruta förblir hel.

Tomas Tranströmer, born in 1931, is a leading Swedish poet. His poetry has been translated into more than sixty languages. His works in English include the collections *Hemligheter på vägen* (1958; Secrets along the way), *Den halvfärdiga himlen* (1962; *The Half-Finished Heaven*, 2001), *Klanger och spår* (1966; see *Windows & Stones: Selected Poems*, 1972), *Östersjöar* (1974; *Baltics*, 1975), *Sorgegondolen* (1996; *The Sorrow Gondola*, 1997), and *Den stora gåtan* (2004; *The Great Enigma*, 2006). He is fully represented in *New Collected Poems*, translated by Robin Fulton (Bloodaxe Books 2011). Tranströmer has himself translated poetry into Swedish from other languages. In 2011 The Swedish Academy awarded Tomas Tranströmer the Nobel Prize for Literature 'because, through his condensed, translucent images, he gives us fresh access to reality'.

Ingar Palmlund is a writer who lives in London. Given a pocket edition of Palgrave's *Golden Treasury* for her fifteenth birthday, she fell in love with the music and imagery in Keats' and Wordsworth's poems. She lectures regularly on international environmental policy and sustainable development at Tufts University, USA. She has published several books and numerous articles, mainly non-fiction, in English and Swedish.

Ingar writes:
Some poems are instant pleasures, delights to discover and enjoy for a while. Others are poems to live by. Tomas Tranströmer's 'Allegro' is one of those. For years I have kept it in my desk drawer to look at when in need. It speaks of liberty but also of integrity, individuality and persistence in spite of headwinds.

I live between languages. Some years ago I made my first English version of 'Allegro', but something subtle in the music and elegance got lost. *MPT*'s invitation to submit poems on the theme of freedom prompted another go. The compact Oxford thesaurus on my bookshelf helped me reformulate problematic lines. Suddenly all worked – syllables, rhythm, and meanings.

Second Prize

A translation by Julia Sanches of Guto Leite's 'Mercado'.

Market

the old men do not pose with pride
less so the old black men

with their mended clothing
their cardboard price signs
their colourful textiles
their dirty iron eyes
and their foreign hats
framing the contours of their heads

the ceramics the shade of skin
are shattered and buried

the new blacks who pose
with fear of the old whites

Mercado

os velhos não posam com orgulho
menos os velhos pretos

com suas vestes preservadas
suas tabuletas de preço
seus tecidos coloridos
seus olhos sujos de ferro
com chapéus expatriados
dando contorno à cabeça

da cor da pele as cerâmicas
se espatifam se enterram

os novos pretos que posam
com medo dos brancos velhos

Guto Leite is a Brazilian poet, author of the books *zero um* (2010), *Poemas Lançados Fora* (7 Letras, 2007), *Sintaxe da Última Hora* (Scortecci, 2006) and *Reflexos* (FEME, 2000). He has also won several literary competitions and has been published in various poetry anthologies. Guto was on the shortlist for the Premio Açoriano in the category of Poetry. He co-wrote the scripts for *Estado Senil* (2009), *Revés* (2008), and *Bons sonhos, Maria* (2006). He is the scriptwriter for the character Júlio César, published in September 2010 in the magazine *Eixada* and in July 2011 in the collection *O melhor da festa*, volume 3. He is a linguist (Unicamp), and has a doctorate in Brazilian Literature (UFRGS). He is currently working as a temporary professor in Brazilian Literature in UFRGS. www.gutoleite.com.br

Julia Sanches is Brazilian by birth but has lived in New York, Mexico City, Lausanne, Edinburgh and Barcelona. She is currently studying Comparative Literature and Literary Translation at UPF in Barcelona. She completed her M.A. in Philosophy and English Literature at the University of Edinburgh in Scotland in 2010. She has been nominated for the *Guardian* and the *Herald* Student Media Awards in the category of Best Photographer. While doing her masters, she also works as a freelance translator, private teacher of English and Portuguese, and as a reader for Random House Mondadori. She is currently learning her sixth language and living in her sixth country.

Equal Runners-up

1. A translation by Brian Holton (with Lee Man-Kay) of Jiang
Tao's 《古猿部落》

Tribe of Palaeopithecus

the forest was filled with fallen fruit, a scarlet carpet
whose origin lay in geological change
the waters had receded, the tiger's sabre tooth was rotten
around the empty ground we discussed the future
the old ones had just crawled out from evolution, waving
    their old fists
the young ones could no longer hold their tongues, they'd got
    to be the first
to eat the sika deer: ambition to move a mountain lacking
though they could ford the river, north and south
the fields were just a dining table
the so-called republic too rumbustious
nevertheless autumn's despotism drove off mosquitoes and
    flies
fortunately we were all standing upright
able to watch the stars, fight empty-handed to free ourselves
    from the food chain
but the October work force
still inclined towards surplus: no need to paint our skin, or to
    cook
with flesh for firewood, only the males kept on
up-ending the females, chanting the beauty of it
until, at least with spring flowers and autumn moons,
to say 'I love you' out loud still took two million years

《古猿部落》

树林里落满果实，猩红的地毯

关于地质的变迁

水退了，老虎的剑齿烂了

我们围着空地商量未来

绿的刚从进化里爬出，挥老拳

小的已按耐不住舌头，要第一个

先吃梅花鹿，移山的志向没有

则可以·水，南方北方的

田野只是一张餐桌

所谓共和闹哄哄

还是独裁之秋赶走蚊蝇

好在我们都直立着

可以观天象，徒手挣脱了食物链

是十月的劳动力

还是倾向剩余：不需要画皮，烹饪

自身当木柴，只有公的继续

把母的掀翻，朗诵袍的美

还要说出"我爱你"

缺少春花秋月的，还要两百万年

Jiang Tao was born in Tianjin in 1970, and studied first at
Tsinghua University, only to abandon biomedical engineering for
a PhD in Chinese literature at Peking University, where he began
teaching in 2002. He wrote poetry as a student, and was editor of
the folk poetry journals *Offset* and *Poetry Communications*. His first
collection *Bird Sutras* was published by Shanghai Joint Publishing
in 2005, and he has also printed and published *Four Poems* and
Mourning for Sometimes. He won the Liu Li'an Prize for Poetry
in 1997. As well as poetry, criticism and historical research, his
doctoral dissertation, 'An Anthology of New Verse' *and the Rise*

of Modern Poetry in China (Peking University Press, 2005), won the National Award for Excellence in Doctoral Dissertations. In addition, he has translated Marston Anderson's *The Limits to Realism: Chinese Fiction in the Revolutionary Period* (Jiangsu People's Publishing House, 2001), and edited *The Beijing University Literary Forum* (Central Compilation and Translation Press, 2005), and the high school language textbook *The Appreciation of Foreign Poetry & Prose* (People's Education Press, 2005).

Brian Holton studied Chinese at Edinburgh and Durham: he has taught at both universities as well as at Newcastle, where he was the first director of the Translating & Interpreting programme; after that he spent nine years teaching translation in Hong Kong. He has published many translations of Chinese literature into English and into his native Scots, as well as articles and essays on translation. Beginning in 1994, he has translated several books by the poet Yang Lian, and has collaborated with Yang and WN Herbert on the forthcoming Bloodaxe anthology *Jade Ladder: Contemporary Chinese Poetry* in which 'Tribe of Palaeopithecus' appears.

Brian writes:
How to make a poem something more than an assembly of unrelated lines? That's the challenge that faces every translator of poetry: what are the hidden springs that will make your 'contraption of words' hum? Jiang Tao's poem looked at first sight as if it were simply the free verse that is the default mode for much contemporary Chinese poetry, but it proved to have a delicately set-out and understated rhyme scheme, and the sort of conversational iambic rhythm into which Chinese naturally falls. Now, Chinese rhymes much more readily than English does, and it is all too easy to mangle a Chinese poem by forcing it into a rhyme scheme, with results which are beyond parody. I chose to use a rhythm which aimed to be natural yet slightly tighter than normal conversation, and I chose alliteration as my main cohesive tool. There is an F-structure that begins with a bang in line 1,

and fades away as we go through the poem, to be replaced by the M-structure which begins in line 4 and reaches its climax in line 19, and there are other more local alliterations, and more dispersed T-, L-, S-, and N-structures, all of which work to bind the lines together into a musical unit. (Robert Louis Stevenson's essay 'On Some Technical Elements of Style in Literature' is the essential reference for translators considering the musicality of English.)

The first drafts, the interrogation of Jiang Tao's text – 'Could it mean *this?*' – were done with the talented young Hong Kong translator Lee Man-Kay, who produced the first literal; our work was then dissected by the poet Yang Lian, a master of his craft: his job was to ensure our English poem didn't stray too far from Jiang Tao's. I then took over the task of polishing the revised draft into a functioning poem, and I was aided in the final stages of this by the Dundee poet W.N. Herbert, who cast his devilishly ingenious eye over my work, and made helpful suggestions. I thank all three of them here: the final English poem bears all their fingerprints.

2. A translation by Clare Pollard of Agnieszka Wolny-Hamkało's 'życiorys.fm'

FM-Biography

Such stories happen on the road –
the hitchhiker says: 'wherever'
and you know where. There's an easier way, there are
such places: pools of spilt light cool as billycans,
the snail-slow pulse of passing towns. Night
tastes of arsenic, mint. My friend-from-nowhere, when I was
    small
I washed my hair with lemon soap, witnessed spirits
on flyovers, out-of-this-world. And here, on radio,
biographies get written: 'weather forecast for night travellers'.
    We get it:

tomorrow's sun will be plush
and strewn. Corn's ears burn, a quiet
crackle, with the ladybirds, grasshoppers,
dill's white scraps. The seasons's ending. After us,
brother, after us, the flood.

życiorys.fm

Zdarzają się takie historie na trasie:
autostopowicz mówi: 'gdziekolwiek',
a ty wiesz dokąd. Jest takie łagodne przejście, są
takie miejsca: rozlewiska świateł chłodne jak menażki,
niespieszne tętna mijanych miasteczek. Noc tam
smakuje arszenikiem, miętą. Znikąd-mój-przyacielu, kiedy
      byłam mała
myłam włosy cytrynowym mydłem, na wiaduktach
widywałam zjawy nie-z-tej-ziemi. A tu UKF – życiorys
się pisze: prognoza pogody dla 'podróżujących
nocą'. Załapujemy: jutrzejsze słońce będzie w weluru
i rozstrzelane. Kolby kukurydzy płoną już
z cichym trzaskiem, i biedronki, pasikoniki,
białe ścinki suchego kopru. Kończy się sezon, po nas,
braciszku, po nas choćby potocznie.

Agnieszka Wolny-Hamkało, born in 1979, a poet and journalist, living in Warsaw. She has published six books of poetry: *Mocno poszukiwana* (*Most wanted*, 1999), *Lonty* (*Fuses*, 2001), *Gospel* (2004), *Ani mi się śni* (*No way, I will*, 2006), *Spamy miłosne* (*Spams of love* 2007) and *Nikon i Leica* (2010). She has also published two books for children: *Nochal Czarodziej* (*Nochal the Wizzard*) and *O tym jak paw wpadł w staw* (*How the peacock fell into the lake*). Her poems have been translated into English, Russian, Ukrainian, Italian, Chinese, Hungarian, German, Swedish, Danish, Czech, Spanish, Serbian, Slovak, and French.

Agnieszka Wolny-Hamkało is widely present in anthologies of young Polish poetry and she regularly publishes poems and essays in magazines. Her particular interests and expertise are in cultural studies, multimedia and feminist art. She is also a teacher on creative writing courses.

Clare Pollard has published four collections of poetry, the most recent of which, *Changeling* (Bloodaxe, 2011), is a Poetry Book Society Recommendation. Her play *The Weather* premiered at the Royal Court Theatre and her documentary for radio, *My Male Muse*, was a Radio 4 Pick of the Year. She has recently co-translated a chapbook of poems by the Somalian poet Caasha Luul Mohamad Yusuf (Poetry Translation Centre, 2012) and her new version of Ovid's *Heroides* will be published by Bloodaxe in 2013.

Clare writes:
I translated this poem as part of the 'Visegrád Poets' Project. It involved a female poet from each of the Visegrád countries, along with German and English poets. The participants were myself, Anna T Szabo (Hungary), Agnieszka Wolny-Hamkało (Poland), Katerina Rudcenkova (Czech), Katarina Kucbelova (Slovakia) and Nora Gomringer (Germany). We spent a week in Hungary, first at the wonderful translators' house by Lake Balaton, where we worked intensively for a few days translating each other's poems, then in Budapest for a reading where we unveiled our translations. Fortunately for me, the translation sessions were carried out in our common language, English. We would listen to one of the poets read their poem a couple of times, enjoying the language, and then talk through the poem line-by-line, getting a sense of what the poet meant and asking lots of questions. It would take at least a couple of hours for each poem – especially as we kept getting distracted by delicious Balaton wine, discussions about men and politics, and Anna's Hungarian hospitality as she whipped up another plate of delicious snacks. After this, we'd retire to our rooms, dictionaries by our sides, and try to turn our notes into a living poem.

I loved Agnieszka's 'FM Biography' immediately. Agnieszka is such a free spirit, and the poem has a real wildness – Beat poetry brought to contemporary Poland. I hope that spending a week with her helped me to capture her distinct voice!

3. A translation by Allen Prowle of Antonio Machado's 'Amenecer en Valencia. Desde Una Torre'

Dawn in Valencia
From a tower

These March winds gusting in the attics –
looking towards the sea – of time; the dove
with lustrous feathers; the tulips
gigantic in the garden, and the sun high above,

through the mist a ball of fire
flooding the Levantine land with its light.
A seething of milk and silver, indigo and surf,
and white sails upon the Latin sea!

Valencia of fecund spring times,
of gardens in bloom and fields of rice,
I want to sing of you in joy, as you used to be,

binding a wide river in your canals,
the sea god with your lagoons,
the centaur of love with your roses.

Amenecer en Valencia
Desde Una Torre

Estas rachas de marzo, en los desvanes
-hacia la mar- del tiempo; la paloma
de pluma tornasol, los tulipanes
gigantes del jardín, y el sol que asoma

bola de fuego entre morada bruma,
a iluminar la tierra levantina...
¡Hervor de leche y plata, añil y espuma,
y velas blancas en la mar latina!

Valencia de fecundas primaveras,
de floridas almunias y arrozales,
feliz quiero cantarte, como eras,

domando a un ancho río en tus canales,
al díos marino con tus albuferas,
al centauro de amor con tus rosales.

Antonio Machado (1875–1939) was one of the foremost figures
of the Spanish literary movement known as the 'generation of
'98'. His early poems were in tune with those of his European
'fin de siècle' contemporaries, introspective and melancholy
meditations on time and memory. Later he moved to a more
critical, often uncompromising, contemplation of what had led to
Spain's decline, exploring its divisions in the hope of recovering
the unity that had supported its former greatness. He was an
ardent supporter of the Second Spanish Republic proclaimed in
1931, contributing newspaper articles in defence of its political
programme. After Franco's coup he was forced to leave Madrid
for Valencia, and then, although in very poor health, to cross

the Pyrenees into France. He died of exhaustion in Collioure; his mother, who had accompanied him, died a few days later.

Allen Prowle was awarded the Times/Stephen Spender Prize 2007 for his translations of poems by Attilio Bertolucci. Previously, the Lincolnshire Association commissioned his translations of poems by Paul Verlaine to commemorate the centenary of the poet's residence in Stickney in 1875. A collection of his own poems, *Landmarks*, appeared in 1977. He is the translator of the first *MPT* Poets pamphlet, Rocco Scotellaro, *Poems*, published in 2009.

Allen writes:

'Dawn in Valencia' is one of nine sonnets which appeared together in the June 1938 issue of the republican journal, *Hora de España*, based in Valencia.I knew from somewhere in the back of my mind that Machado had written poems during and about the civil war, but they never seemed to surface in any of the collections I had read. It was a double surprise eventually to 'unearth' these: not only were they not sporadic, they formed a unified sequence in themselves; also, the chosen form was one I had not seen in his work before. It was a time of terrible upheaval and violence, but Machado recreates the Valencia of his mind and memory and holds it within the secure formal containment of the sonnet, an emblem of devotion and defiance.

Commendation

The judges also wish to commend **Marie Naughton** for her translation of Zbigniew Herbert's 'Nigdy o tobie' ('Never you').

Acknowledgements

We are grateful to the publishers of Tomas Tranströmer, Guto Leite, Jiang Tao and Agnieszka Wolny-Hamkało for allowing us to publish the original poems with their translations. Copyright of those poems rests with the authors.

Reviews

Poems from Other Tongues
Translated by Michael Smith and Luis Ingelmo
Shearsman Books, 2011
Paperback, 105pp, £9.95, ISBN 9781848611344

Manannan's Cloak A Bilingual Anthology of Manx Literature
Selected and translated by Robert Corteen Carswell
Francis Boutle Publishers, 2011
Paperback 235pp, £16.99, ISBN 9781903427491

The theorist Bakhtin claimed that laughter in its various forms is one of the 'least scrutinized' modes of expression. In *Poems from Other Tongues*, which includes translations from the Greek, Latin, Andalusian Arabic and Irish, the translators describe the 1st century B.C. Greek Love Poems as 'a kind of laughter in the bright air'. The poems make exuberant, playful attempts to defy time, clearly aware of that impossibility, and almost succeed through our ability to access them. Philodemos argues in 'Late Beauty' that 'Lovers, unfearful, driven by desire / ...take no heed of years.' In 'Autumn Beauty', Silentiarius claims 'Your autumn's richer than another's spring; / your winter more than others' summer heat.' The anonymous poem 'Fruit of the Vine' pleads: 'A green grape, you rejected me./ Ripe, you warned me off./ But now at least/ allow me a little raisin.' In 'Asian Dancing-Girl' by Automedon, 'Her thigh upon the rudder / raises it from death.' In Meleager's 'Morning Star', unrequited love stalls time: 'now someone else lies snug in Demo's bed / how slow around the earth your revolutions are.' These translations sound urgent and fresh, as if the poems themselves have sought to escape mortality through a humorously erotic life force. Similarly, in the much shorter Latin section, a poem by Propertius reads like one of Donne's metaphysical seductions: 'What sense, my love, coquettish bustle/../ When Love himself / despises all but natural pelt!'

The Andalusian Arabic poems are created from Spanish versions with the collaboration of Luis Ingelmo, originally composed as *ghazals* and *qasidas*, which reportedly influenced Lorca's work. Mainly written between the eleventh and thirteenth centuries, around the time Christian crusaders were reconquering Spain, the sensuous imagery frequently has political undertones. In 'The Young Pigeon' by Abu al-Hasan, the bird is 'perching on the arak branch like a throne, / hiding its throat in the fold of its wing.' In King Mu'tamid of Seville's 'Evocation of Silves': 'The strings of her lute wounded by the plectrum / made me tremble / as if hearing the melody of swords / in the tendons of an enemy's neck.' Ibn Sara of Santarén's 'A Reservoir with Turtles' makes a direct, apparently lighthearted reference to the crusaders:

> In it there are turtles whose leaps in the water amuse me
> and that are enveloped in clothes of scum
> . . .
> And if at any time they peep up in their games,
> they resemble Christian soldiers
> who bear on their shoulders shields of suede.

The Irish poems, mostly anonymous, are dated between the mid-fourteenth and mid-eighteen centuries. The book closes with a powerful ballad, 'The Adventures of the Magic Cloak', which mocks both male sexuality and female chastity. With grotesque realism, the cloak exposes to a group of men the infidelity of their wives, who are consequently killed by their husbands or flee the scene.

Mannanan's Cloak provides us with a comprehensive overview of written and oral traditions on the Isle of Man. It traces the Manx language's Gaelic origins, its re-emergence after Scandinavian rule, suppression with the rise of the British Empire, and a grass roots revival, leading to its inclusion on the school curriculum today. This braided history of Manx literature includes the mythical 'Fin and Oshin' from the early Ossianic oral tradition, ballads, carvals (carols), gospels and hymns, as well as translations from Aesop's Fables, Tennyson's 'Morte

D'Arthur', 'Paradise Lost' and the Rubaiyat. The texts, along with the commentary, help to illustrate an historical 'tug of war' between imperialistic claims for a unified national identity – often in religious guise – and dissenting voices keen to keep the Manx language alive.

The cloak of the title is a mist protecting the Isle of Man from outsiders. 'The Traditionary Ballad' from the late fifteenth/early sixteenth-century recounts the myth. In a mid-nineteenth-century poem by William Kennish called 'Lamenting the Mother Tongue of the Isle of Man', the language of Manx is personified by a woman in tatters:

. . . honnick me ben voght ayns coamrey glass	. . . I saw a poor woman in grey clothing Coming to meet me amongst the heather
Cheet my-whail ny mastey yn freoagh	With all about her ragged and ripped
Lesh ooilley mygeayrt-y-mooie frytlagh as rasst	Running as if she were maddened
Roie myr dy beagh ee er-keoiagh	

Other memorable texts include the early eighteenth-century 'Carval of Bad Women', perhaps one of the more extreme attempts to control behaviour through the church. Conversely, Neddy Beg's early twentieth-century translation of the fable 'The Wolf and The Lamb' into Manx-Gaelic carries a strong anti-establishment message. In John Moore's late eighteenth-century poem, 'The Voyage of the Tiger', a man goes to war on behalf of the empire but – wistful of time passing – eventually turns away from England and returns to his true love on Mannin. In this extract, Moore's original in Manx allows us to sense more fully its emotional as well as political impact.

O shiuish my gheiney cheerey	O you my countrymen
Ta geaishtagh rish m'arrane,	Who are listening to my song
My choyrle te diu ve creeney,	My advice to you is to be wise
Choud's ta'n traa er-mayrn.	Whilst there's time remaining
She'n chooish ta ooilley lhie er,	It's the thing that everything depends on
Dy ghoaill kiarail ayns traa,	To watch out in time
Roish bee laa'n vargee harrish,	Before the market day will be over
Nyn drimshey son dy braa.	Our sorrow forever

The two anthologies highlight different approaches to the task of translating from languages that are either 'dead' or being revived.

Manannan's Cloak, containing prose as well as verse, is occasionally of more historical than literary interest; however, we are well served with both Manx and English versions of the texts. The background text helps us to consider wider issues surrounding minority languages and cultures. *Poems from Other Tongues* provides little context, and yet the translated poems themselves also reflect very contemporary concerns. In both collections, universal themes of love and death are explored alongside dynamics of domination and resistance. In turn, the struggles for self-identity point to more fundamental concerns of the human spirit.

Janet Kofi-Tsekpo

Alfonso Gatto
The Wall Did Not Answer: Selected Poems 1932–1976
Translated and introduced by Philip Parisi
Chelsea Editions 2011
Paperback, 229pp $20 **ISBN** 9870982384961

Pierre-Albert Jourdan
The Straw Sandals: Selected Prose and Poetry
Edited, introduced and translated by John Taylor
Chelsea Editions 2011
Paperback, 332pp $20 **ISBN** 9780982384985

Chelsea Editions is a small New York press whose editor, Alfredo de Palchi, is dedicated to making available in English a range of Italian poets from the twentieth and twenty-first centuries, beyond already famous names like Montale, Quasimodo, and Ungaretti. Chelsea publishes parallel text editions of sixteen 'modern and contemporary' Italian poets, and as a bonus, editions of two French writers, both translated by John Taylor: Philippe Jaccottet and Pierre-Albert Jourdan.

Alfonso Gatto (1909–1976) has been a well-known poet in Italy ever since his first volume *Isola* ('Island,' 1932) was greeted as evidence of a major new talent by Eugenio Montale among others. During the Fascist period he was a member of the resistance, and was imprisoned for six months in 1936. After the end of the war he was a prominent figure in Italian literature and politics until his death in a car accident in 1976. He is buried in his native Salerno, where his grave is marked by a boulder bearing this epitaph by Montale: 'Alfonso Gatto – for whom poetry and life were one single testament of love.'

These words point to the heart of the poetry's thematic concerns. Gatto's poems often focus on the dispossessed, the poor, and the marginalized: troubled children, bereaved mothers, or victims of wartime massacres. Given this concern with the victims of history (like many in his generation, he was for a time a member of the Italian Communist party), we might expect a politicized approach to poetry, with indignation leading to calls for action. Instead we find a highly subjective and sometimes obscure style influenced by the French symbolists as well as by Italian 'hermeticists' like Ungaretti and Montale.

Many of Gatto's poems have an evocatively rendered landscape setting, rural or urban. The time is often at dawn, or (less often) at evening, when the proximity of night leads naturally to reflections on the dead: 'Italy/ is a poor land where man/ is born with the dead,' he writes in 'To a Stranger.' These meditations on mortality sometimes rise towards a denouement that is coloured by Christianity as much as by Marxism: they envision an apocalyptic uprising of the 'radiant multitude' from death, and a triumph over their oppression in life. Gatto's poems attempt to find a consolatory meaning in the suffering of victims; they are acts of commemoration as well as questionings of an unjust world.

The notion of a 'sign' recurs in many poems, linking their human content with their poetic technique. They attempt to find in suffering a sign 'for something that will come,' to use the title of what could be Gatto's most significant poem. 'The victim's footprint appears to be disappearing,' he writes here; but this event could be 'the sign of disappearing/ in the completed work.' The 'completed work' could be both the end of a life of suffering and the poem which commemorates it. Gatto uses both narration and description to search individual or collective experience to discover a symbol that could be seen as redemptive. Gatto is known as a poet of resistance (in several senses of that word), but acceptance at times seems to fuse with it: he can talk of 'beautiful death' in a way reminiscent of Yeats or Rilke.

At his most intense he can fuse the religious and the political in a moving way: 'We pray now that nothing be dissolved,/ that the life of the dead and ours bond together/ deep within us.' The bleak outlook implied by this selection's title ('the wall did not answer' is the last phrase in the poem 'An Evening in March') is normally not the final attitude taken by Gatto's reflections on death and injustice: more often there is a note of prophetic anticipation, for example, of 'one day/ [when] Italy will sing among the people/ of the opened tombs.' Resistance may lead to defeat and death, but may eventually be vindicated by resurrection. Fittingly, this volume ends with a poem devoted to Lazarus.

Philip Parisi has done an excellent job of rendering these poems into a flexible, idiomatic English that reads well without simplifying or explaining the obscurities, paradoxes and intuitive leaps of the Italian.

Pierre-Albert Jourdan (1924–1981) did not have a typical literary career. He worked in the insurance industry, and, though based in Paris, preferred to spend his time in his native Provence, at his country home in Caromb in the Vaucluse. He had few literary connections until late in his life, and much of his work was published posthumously. His premature death was caused by lung cancer.

His writings are hard to classify, but perhaps 'notes' is the best term to cover the wide variety of short pieces (between a paragraph and a few words in length) that make up his books: journal entries, observations of nature, aphorisms, sentence fragments, quotations, vignettes, and so on. Occasionally he is reminiscent of philosophers like Cioran or Nietzsche, whose preferred unit is the paragraph; at other times, he resembles aphorists like La Rochefoucauld or Pascal, who often confine their thoughts to one or two sentences. It would also be misleading to classify Jourdan as a nature writer. There is little description as such, and no panoramic views, accounts of walks, or anecdotes from local history. Instead, Jourdan singles out an object – a named plant or bird, a small incident – then gives a reflection of it, or on it, then nothing further. Perhaps his books belong most in the tradition of 'notebooks' or 'cahiers,' an informal genre seemingly more accepted in continental Europe than in the English-speaking world. Where Jourdan differs is that these notebooks are his principal works, not a supplement to major poems or novels, as in the case of more famous writers like Valéry or Gide.

The distinction between poetry and prose seems to collapse in

Jourdan's writing, but the term 'prose poems' in the Baudelairean sense misses the mark. His fragments are more like 'pre-poems' – observations that a poet would likely consider raw material to be developed into a poem – but Jourdan prefers the rawness to the development. He prizes the first inklings of a thought or sensation, and tries to catch the earliest state of these awarenesses, before they are connected up into chains of reasoning or narrative. These are the 'immediate givens of consciousness,' insofar as they can be caught in language at all. They seem to be jotted down at the moment they emerge from the unknown.

Jourdan describes the excitement that fills him at the sight of maxims like La Rochefoucauld's, hoping for 'flashes of lightning that will illuminate the darkest night'. But then he continues, 'We must not forget that a tree, a hill, or a flower can offer us equally intense maxims' ('sentences' in French). Where La Rochefoucauld's focus is on human nature, Jourdan's is on nature; and where La Rochefoucauld's mode is analysis, Jourdan's is receptivity. He aims to listen to and record what Nature offers. The emphasis is on receiving, not creating – this humility (which he once links etymologically to *humus*, earth, and hence humanity) separates him from the Romantic stress on human creativity, and also from the lyrical eloquence of the Modernist prose epiphany as found in Joyce, Woolf or Proust. Jourdan's writing exemplifies bareness and brevity. Speaking of his native landscape in Provence, he writes, 'When I wrote, I took down its dictation.' The idea is 'to live for a single moment the truth of this branch.' Once he calls his fragments 'peelings'. Their aim is not to develop the self, as in much Romantic nature writing, but to dissolve it: 'Forget me, so that I too may forget myself.' Absence, emptiness, vanishing, effacing, silence, the void – these are recurrent themes, at times evocative of Zen.

The language of Jourdan's notes is inevitably fragile, their meaning often obscure, attenuated or simply suggestive. John Taylor has generally provided readable versions of the fragments, but there are some jolts where he uses the nearest English cognate words rather than an expression a writer in English would normally use. This can be awkward: 'l'heureuse hébétude' becomes 'happy hebetude,' a phrase hard to imagine being used in an English original. Jourdan several times uses this word for a state of mental vacancy or passivity; 'numbness' or 'dullness' or 'stupor' don't completely convey this, but would surely be preferable to using 'hebetude' in English. Other examples: 'douloureuse' becomes 'dolorous' rather than 'gloomy'; 'délicatesse' becomes 'delicacy' rather than 'tact'; 'une lithographie' is rendered 'a lithography' rather than 'a lithograph.' Occasionally this habit of using cognates is actually misleading: 'rudesse' (used of winter's 'cleaning up') is surely 'roughness' rather than 'rudeness,' which in contemporary English usage suggests only social impoliteness. Sometimes French words like 'socle' and 'rutilant' are simply reproduced in the translation; although they occur in the English dictionary, they will puzzle many native speakers. But despite these flaws, we can be thankful to John Taylor and Chelsea Editions for making a fascinating and little-known author available in English.

Graham Good

Cyprian Kamil Norwid
Selected Poems
Translated by Adam Czerniawski
Anvil Press, Second Edition 2011,
Paperback, 104pp, £9.95, ISBN 9780856464379

Tadeusz Różewicz
They Came To See A Poet – Selected Poems
Translated by Adam Czerniawski
Anvil Press, Third Edition 2011,
Paperback, 288pp, £14.95 ISBN 978085646974362 2011

Six Poets Twenty-eight Poems from Sopot
Selected with an introduction by Krzysztof Kuczkowski
Translated by David Malcolm and Jennifer Zielińska
Biblioteka 'Toposu', Sopot, 2011,
Paperback, 79pp, ISBN 9788361002178

After the suppressed Hungarian uprising against Soviet control in 1956, Poland's communist literary weekly published Norwid's elegy 'A Funeral Rhapsody in Memory of Józef Bem' in silent tribute – Józef Bem had been a 19[th-] century general and freedom fighter, a contemporary of the poet. Just over a decade later, during the repressions of 1969 within Poland, the popular singer Czesław Niemen recorded a progressive rock version of this poem. Such is the resonance of Norwid's work. He is one of Poland's leading Romantic poets with Mickiewicz and Słowacki, his poems learnt by heart in school.

Yet during his lifetime Norwid, owing to the individual and non-conformist style of his work, was little understood or published. Born near Warsaw in 1821 he died in 1883 in obscurity in Paris, a tragic figure having spent much of his life in exile, poverty-stricken and isolated.

His rhyme schemes and diminutives alone pose instant problems for a translator – challenges Czerniawski freely admits to, making clean, well-crafted translations. Norwid's insistence on conciseness, using colloquial speech while being drawn to classical themes and writing in parables and metaphors, earned him the reputation of being obscure; his realist-romantic style deemed too modern. With remarkable prescience he wrote that his 'songs' would be 'spurned' in his own time, understood only by future generations – 'grandsons' – once 'the epoch's chill is gone'.

However Norwid wanted to know not only how he might be received but what endures of any human endeavour. In 'Memento' he conjures up a ruined castle with immense oak doors:

> Shaped like an eagle hammered out of nails
> So when the wind rushing through the terrace
>
> Swung the massive portals,
> The eagle torn in half swayed to and fro

The eagle – a national symbol –'moans hoarsely', caught by 'nail-gripped wings'. Like other passers-by, the poet hopes to carve something on these oak portals:

> . . . and artfully score my name and crest . . .
> containing *an anchor* or *two doves*
> so that a great historian . . . might recall
> that when I came here . . . I owned a blade.

If Norwid felt himself set apart – 'Why Not In Chorus?' – by his own sharp vision, Różewicz born a century later appears immediately approachable. The poet Anna Świr named his poetry as one of the things to hold onto in your darkest moments. It is not difficult to see why. His poems are dependably clear, uncluttered, and free from illusion. Their depth becomes apparent the more you read them.

Różewicz was eighteen when the Nazi and Soviet armies simultaneously occupied Poland. Like others of his generation he studied at a clandestine school and took part in the Resistance. His writing was born of the experience of ultimate situations and his belief that *poetic* language had no place after the Second World War and the genocide by two totalitarian regimes. In his informative, personal introduction Czerniawski explains he has been at pains to point out the breadth of Różewicz's thematic range to those who think of him as a war poet, though the impact of early poems like 'Pigtail' about the Auschwitz museum or 'The Survivor' is undeniable.

Różewicz became a master of *anti-poetry* in his quest for transparency and his rejection of artistic posturing. He relished the influence of Norwid, whose laconic style he admired. Różewicz's writing could also be said to contain a *naming of objects* – grass, rope, brick and, like Norwid, he often wrote about the act of making poetry itself.

My poetry

Explains nothing
Clarifies nothing
Makes no sacrifices
Is not all-embracing
Doesn't fulfil any hopes . . .

If it's not a cryptic language
if it speaks without originality

if it doesn't surprise
evidently that's how things must be . . .

('My Poetry')

Where Miłosz, born a decade earlier than Różewicz, saw his role as witness or mediator of the events and lost worlds of the twentieth century, Różewicz is more concerned to show the moment of rupture or heart-break and dislocation itself. He is also always trying to find ways to build, later even 'recycle' his own world; the 'Doors' of his childhood take him back, ultimately, to a point of nothingness.

It is a monumental achievement that Adam Czerniawski has selected and translated Różewicz's poems into English providing such a broad overview of the poet's work from 1947 to 2004 – a triumph that the book has gone to third edition with further additions, while simultaneously his translations of Norwid are also reprinted. My only regret is that the publisher could not provide dual language versions, a sign, surely, of the cutting times poetry is in.

These giant stars, Norwid and Różewicz, will undoubtedly have made an impact on all Six Sopot poets, born between the 1950s and the 1980's. In his editor's preface Kuczkowski says the anthology is not intended as an exhaustive representation only a 'pleiad' 'in the starry firmament of contemporary Polish verse'. All the poets are linked to the seaside town of Sopot, site of the International Literary Festival – Back 2 – and the journal Topos. What jars is the unavowed omission of women poets. This does not serve the promotion of Polish poetry well.

Having said that, the voices in this book are spirited, edgy and engaging. Some – like Dąbrowski – are already known in the U.K, others are newer to this readership. Many poems employ a street-wise vernacular – an *anti-poetry* of everyday microcosms, while not eschewing lyricism, like Kass's tender boy/lamb with his 'bell of genitals' in 'I ran from that dream'. In places uneven, the American translations offer some ingenious takes on colloquialisms. There is much that shines: Mansztajn's tough urban rhetoric which belies his sensibility, Dąbrowski's wit in his 'Lover's Discourse' on infidelity, Kuczkowski's *rouge et noir*, Więcek's sci-fi prayer or – neatly echoing Dąbrowski's 'Resolution' – Nowaczewski's 'Commodore 64':

> just because they increase the resolution
> doesn't necessarily mean you see more.
> I'm opening my childhood and there:
> the computer has 64kB of memory

a poem ending in – for me, a typically Polish – celebration of everything
underrated:

> . . . who'll understand,
> that poor graphics were close
>
> to the invisible.

   ('Commodore 64')

Maria Jastrzębska

Further Reviews

The Songs of António Botto
Translated by Fernando Pessoa
Edited by Josiah Blackmore
University of Minnesota Press
Paperback, 168pp $17.95 ISBN 10081667101X

Beautiful Words: Kasuundze' Kenaege': The Complete Ahtna Poems
Poems and translations by **John Elvis Smelcer**
Truman State University Press 2011
Paperback, 84pp, $16.95 ISBN 9781935503927

János Pilinszky
Passio
Translated from the Hungarian by George Gömöri and Clive Wilmer
Worple Press.
Paperback, 20pp, £6.95 ISBN 9781905208159

Ingeborg Bachmann
Enigma. Selected Poems
Translated by Mike Lyons and Patrick Drysdale
Ariadne Press
Paperback 132pp ISBN 9781572411814

In this edition of the 'Songs of António Botto' Josiah Blackmore presents Fernando Pessoa's English translations of *Canções*, privately printed in 1948 as *Songs*. The publication of Botto's *Canções* in the 1920s caused a scandal – and provoked a serious debate about the treatment of same-sex desire in Portuguese literature, but also both widespread condemnation and an increasing admiration of Botto's early modernist lyricism.

Botto's work dispenses with internal and external censorship. An unmistakably self-defined voice is present throughout. Each poem is housed within a discrete sequence, opening lines act as urgent invitations: 'No, let us kiss, only kiss/ In this evening's agony.' The

poems in 'Boy' rise up with uncompromising candour, whereas in
'Small Sculptures' the last lines close with a defiant cadence: 'Love
never really lies:/ It simply exaggerates.'

The cinematic 'Olympiad' sequence turns the public sporting arena
into an intimate space. The poems have a contemporary voyeuristic
pose. Botto's writing is a delicate balancing act. He has a quick mind
and an ecstatic eye. The male gaze is liberated: to consider the beauty
of men. Each deliberately enjambed line gives permission to the reader,
regardless of gender, to gaze unashamedly, as one man at another:

> Almost naked,
> Springy
> Dark
> With a gesture
> Full of litheness and of sway,
> He raised the disc in his arms,
> And the disc
> Went off
> Nobly thrown
> In a large and manly way.
>
> In his eyes,
> Very soft and very big
> An expression
> Of weariness and of sin
> Became keener,
> Became clearer
> When he noticed I was looking.

Josiah Blackmore's illuminating introductory essay goes beyond any
compartmentalisation and social interpretation of Botto's sexuality and
aesthetics, and instead considers the poetry, the 'complicated fluidity
between the visual and visceral, between outer form and inner life'.
Botto is, for him, a poet of 'physical and emotional desire, a poet of the
male body'. Pessoa, himself Botto's close friend and champion, thought
him an aesthete in pursuit of Hellenic ideals, a creator. Botto writes
(in 'Curiosity'):

The most important thing in life
Is to create – to create beauty.

To do that
We must foresee it
Where our eyes cannot really see it.

I think that dreaming the impossible
Is like hearing the faint voice
Of something that wants to live
And calls to us from afar.

Yes, the most important thing in life
Is to create.

And we must move
Towards the impossible
With shut eyes, like faith or love.

Botto's vision defies categorisation; his poetry is a breathing memoir. The poems affirm that the necessary act of creating beauty is inseparable from love, inseparable from desire. In this erudite edition of António Botto's poetry, Josiah Blackmore has compassionately 'recuperated and resuscitated modern Portugal's most famous unknown poet'.

Beautiful Words: Kasuundze' Kenaege' is the culmination of many years active listening and a steady commitment to the preservation of the Ahtna Athabaskan language, one of twenty indigenous languages of Alaska, which, according to mythology, was handed down by the Raven. John Smelcer's work was first brought to the attention of readers by Ted Hughes who published the chapbook *Raven Speaks* in 1997.

The Complete Ahtna bilingual Poems forms part of the legacy of Ahtna culture. A vast undertaking for Smelcer, whose first task was to rescue the language from oblivion, to do painstaking research, collating and editing a dictionary and grammar for the Ahtna Heritage Foundation which involved travelling to villages across Alaska gathering pieces of language, word by word, as well as traditional myths and recollections. This culminated in Smelcer becoming a living repository of the language, carrying not only the cultural memory of Ahtna but also its future, for he is one of its last speakers and writers.

The book has Forewords by Steven Pinker and Noam Chomsky and a moving introduction by Smelcer himself, who explores the cultural responsibility, so close to his heart, in 'The Poet': 'I am beginning to write in our language,/ but it is difficult. / Only elders speak our words, / and they are forgetting . . .'

The loss of any language carries with it a loss of self, a loss of existence. The poignancy of these poems lies in the fear that dreaming and imagining in Athna will cease. The poems abound in folklore, song, subtle humour, and critical reflections on nationhood. Reading them is like walking though a disappearing landscape of voices, who were not fit enough or ruthless enough in the competition for survival. The land itself is at the centre of 'Mourning Song for the Last Indian': 'When Indian People are no more/ trees will sing and weep/ mountains will shake/wolves will howl/ and lakes and rivers will go dry.'

(For more Ahtna poems by John Smelcer see *MPT* 3/13 and 3/15.)

Passio is a collection of fourteen poems by János Pilinszky whom Clive Wilmer locates with Paul Celan, Zbigniew Herbert and Yves Bonnefoy in 'an extraordinary generation of poets'; and thinks his war poems an 'overwhelming achievement'. Wilmer's and George Gömöri's motivation for this project was to settle differences with early translations of Pilinszky by Ted Hughes and Janos Coskits (1976). It is impossible not to draw comparisons, especially since Wilmer, in his introduction, insists on making a case against Hughes.

No one can dispute the value of the Hughes/Coskits translations, which are both satisfying and complete in their own right; and yet Wilmer argues that although 'Hughes conveys Pilinszky's images, his nervous anguish and something of his visionary quality with memorable power', it is at the cost 'of abandoning the poetry's cultural halo'. Hughes was aware of his shortcomings. In his illuminating introduction to *The Desert of Love*, he writes: 'in trying to articulate my impression of the key sensations in Pilinszky's poetry, I realise I have ignored important things, and no doubt missed others completely . . . Poems of such symbolic vitality, like cut jewels, draw their light from every direction. But after eight or nine years of acquaintance, it seemed worth the attempt to indicate something of the temper and truth of the vision behind these superficially plain and open poems, to which our translation has directed itself.' Hughes was attracted to 'the air of simple, helpless accuracy' in the poems of Piliniszky whom Wilmer describes as 'a poet who could not posture or tell a lie'.

For Wilmer and Gömöri a chief preoccupation was to reinstate rhyme and metre into the mix, to evoke the folkish ballad, using Blake's 'London' and Coleridge's 'Ancient Mariner' as reference points. Wilmer's ambitious versions achieve an abrupt starkness, signalling Pilinszky's naked vulnerability, the existentialist horror of living through war. Formally, there is an immediacy, a daring bleakness, that echoes Blake's stepped rhythm but not his ease of rhyme. The poem 'The French Prisoner' is a good example of where Wilmer adopts, and is somewhat constrained within, a formal stanza, while Hughes's line is more fluid and felt, and perhaps too open. Translating poems which have such a deep spiritual dimension but whose ultimate remit is to be effortless, the difficulties, and the sacrifices, are many and great.

Wilmer has a great respect for Hughes and it is admirable what has been achieved. There is a freshness to these versions that quiver with a formal tension, Hughes has the steadier hand and reaches into the desolate radiance of the poems, while Wilmer and Gömöri have conveyed Pilinszky as a poet who inhabits suffering deftly, a suffering that cannot be contained even within formal and highly wrought structures but is accentuated by them. Pilinszky, if he were to be found, would be somewhere in between these two very commendable translations.

Enigma (an apt title) draws together poems from Ingeborg Bachmann's first collection *Die gestundete Zeit* alongside later, and even some previously unpublished, work. These lucid translations by Mike Lyons and Patrick Drysdale will widen her readership and are to be welcomed. As Hans Höller says, in his informative Afterword, the poems are as relevant today as they were in the aftermath of World War II. Bachmann is a presiding spirit for our enigmatic times. Despite her established reputation as an innovative modernist of international importance, her work has not always travelled well into English. The reasons are as simple and complex as Bachmann herself, who occupied many spheres, both philosophically and culturally. Alongside her hatred of oppressive structures in post-war Germany and Austria, was a reflective and utopian poetics extending beyond frontiers. Her words of yesterday reach into our world today.

How shall we best meet Ingeborg Bachmann, in which genres? She worked in many forms: radio plays, librettos, short stories, and experimental poetic-prose novels. There are her love poems, and letters to Paul Celan. Her early war diary, translated by Mike Lyons (*MPT* 3/3; and see also 3/14), provides the context of what would become a poetry of resistance to the residues of fascism: 'the absolute complicity of words and images'. Elsewhere, in interview, Bachmann spoke of her disillusionment with poetry: 'I have nothing against poems, but you must try to understand that there are moments when suddenly one has everything against them, against every metaphor, every sound, every rule for putting words together, against the absolutely inspired arrival of words and images.'

These *Selected Poems* are deceptively accessible, which appears to be part of the translators' wish to be faithful to Bachmann's own poetics and to stay 'as close as possible to the meaning of the original and to the forms, and rhythms and general feel of the German verse . . . using simple, everyday words, avoiding any artificial poetic language.' Although Bachmann uses a simple diction in her poetry, the poems contain complexities on many levels: surprises in diction; the poems border on dreamscapes. It is a poetry that imagines in the present tense and reverberates in the future:

> War is no longer declared
> but prolonged. The outrageous
> has become the norm. The hero
> stays far from fighting. The weakling
> has moved into the firing line.
> The day's uniform is patience,
> its medal the wretched star
> of hope above the heart.

(From 'Every Day')

There is an elegant consistency in these translations, so that we may wonder whether Bachmann's highly nuanced reflective style has been sufficiently captured in English. Also, the fraught and often antagonistic relationship between men and women, a contribution to oppressive, and even fascist, politics in Bachmann's view, is less strongly felt in the translation of the iconic poem 'Time on loan' ('Die gestundete Zeit'), than in the German. 'Sand' in German is a masculine noun, so that there might be some sense that a 'he' is harming a female lover:

> Out there your lover's engulfed in sand,
> it climbs around her billowing hair,
> it cuts short her words,
> it tells her to be silent,
> it finds her mortal,
> and ready to part
> after every embrace.

Bachmann's language is indeed fluent, which may explain some discrepancies in translation. The poems do lend themselves to a degree of re-imagining. At their core they need to be experienced, to be felt first, not intellectualized; and an impossible ambition for a translator would be to dissolve the borders of the native German and for English to surrender and transform itself. The courageous efforts of Mike Lyons and Patrick Drysdale provide a valuable insight into the possibilities of Bachmann's work for future readers and translators. As Bachmann herself said, in her Frankfurt Lectures on Poetics (1959–60), 'What actually is possible, however, is transformation. And the transformative effect that emanates from new works leads us to new perception, to a new feeling, new consciousness,'

(For more Bachmann see MPT 3/3, 3/4, 3/11, 3/14.)

Saradha Soobrayen

Notes on Contributors

Born in Gaza, **Atef Alshaer** is a Leverhulme Post-Doctoral Research Fellow in Political Communication and a teaching fellow at SOAS.

Alemu Tebeje Ayele is an Ethiopian poet resident in London and member of the Ethiopian Artists' Association in Britain. He studied Ethiopian Languages & Literature at Addis Ababa University and Journalism at the University of Wales. Among other publications, he is one of the 25 poets to appear in *No Serenity Here: An Anthology of African Poetry* (World Knowledge Publishers, 2010).

Chris Beckett grew up in Ethiopia in the 1960's. He won the *Poetry London* competition in 2001 and his first collection, *The Dog Who Thinks He's A Fish*, appeared in 2004. A collection of praise poems entitled *Ethiopia Boy* is due to be published by Carcanet/ Oxford Poets in Spring 2013.

Martin Bennett lives in Rome where he teaches, proofreads and translates at the University of Tor Vergata.

Richard Berengarten lives in Cambridge. His latest books are *The Blue Butterfly*, *In a Time of Drought*, and *Under Balkan Light* (Shearsman Books). He is currently working on a sequence of poems dedicated to the *Yijing*. His poetry has been translated into more than 90 languages. See: http://interlitq.org/issue9/volta/job.php

Alexander Booth lives and works in Rome. Poems and translations have recently appeared or are forthcoming in *Dear Sir, FreeVerse, halfcircle poetry journal, Italian Poetry Review,* and *Konundrum.* He also volunteers at the historic Non-Catholic Cemetery of Rome and keeps a weblog on Rome in literature and Roman literature, *Misera e stupenda città.*

Tom Cheesman is a Reader in German at Swansea University and runs Hafan Books, raising funds for Swansea Bay Asylum Seekers Support Group. The Hafan list includes his translations from German of poetry and prose by Volker Braun, Ulrike Draesner, Zafer Senocak, and others, and work by Wales-based refugees and experimental poets. See: lulu.com/hafan.

Don Mee Choi is the author of *The Morning News is Exciting* (Action Books, 2010) and has received a 2011 Whiting Writers' Award. She lives and works in Seattle.

Mary-Ann Constantine is a research fellow at the University of Wales. She works on Welsh literature of the Romantic period. Her short stories have appeared in *Planet* and in the *New Welsh Review*.

Victoria Cribb was born in England but spent a number of years travelling, studying and working in Iceland, as a translator, journalist and publisher. Her translations of Icelandic literature include novels by Sjón, Arnaldur Indriðason and Gyrðir Elíasson. She is currently completing a PhD in Old Icelandic literature at Cambridge.

Peter V. Czipott holds a Ph.D. in physics and provides consultation services in applied physics and renewable energy. In collaboration with John Ridland, he has published translations of poems by Miklós Radnóti, Sándor Márai, György Faludy, Bálint Balassi, and Sándor Reményik in journals in the U.S., U.K. and Australia.

Peter Daniels began translating Khodasevich on a Hawthornden Fellowship in 2009; a book of his translations is due from Angel Books in 2013. His own poems have been published in pamphlets with HappenStance and Smith Doorstop, and his first full collection is *Counting Eggs* (Mulfran, 2012).

Julian Farmer is a poet and translator of poetry from a number of languages. Having started with French and then studied Classics, he went on to do Russian and is now exploring a number of Asian languages. His poems and translations have appeared in *Staple*, *Stand*, *Acumen*, *The Shop*, *The London Magazine* and *MPT*.

Kerry Featherstone, after a PhD on Bruce Chatwin, worked in literature development and was then appointed Lecturer in Creative Writing at Loughborough. His research is on globalization and travel-writing, and representations of Afghanistan. He writes poetry in English and French, and is writing a novel set in the Vendée.

Jennie Feldman's new collection of poems, *Swift* (2012) and her translated selections of poems by Jacques Réda, *Treading Lightly* (2005) were published by Anvil, as was *Into the Deep Street: Seven Modern French Poets 1938-2008* (2009), co-edited with Stephen Romer and shortlisted for the Popescu Translation Prize 2011.

Chang Fen-ling received her BA in English from the National Taiwan Normal University. A literary critic and award-winning translator, she has translated, with her husband Chen Li, the work of many poets into Chinese, including Neruda, Paz, Szymborska, Hughes, Larkin, and Heaney.

Maria Grech Ganado (Malta, 1943) studied at the Universities of Malta, Cambridge and Heidelberg, later teaching English literature at the first. She writes poetry in English and Maltese and has translated works by some of Malta's prominent writers, mostly Immanuel Mifsud's poetry. In 2000 she was awarded the Medal for the Service of the Republic for her contribution in education and the arts.

Nene Giorgadze was born Georgia in 1971. She has an MA in Georgian Literature from Ilia University (Tbilisi, Georgia). She has lived in the USA since 1999, and speaks three languages: Georgian, English, and Russian. Her work is forthcoming or has appeared in *Raleigh Review*, *RHINO*, and elsewhere.

Anne-Marie Glasheen: photographer, poet, literary translator. Her father Belgian, mother English, she spent her early childhood in Belgium. A past chair of the Translators Association, in 1998 she won the translation prize awarded annually by the Communauté française de Belgique. Her first collection *Lines in the Sand* was published in 2008.

Graham Good lives in Vancouver, B.C. His volume of translations entitled *Rilke's Late Poetry: Duino Elegies, The Sonnets to Orpheus, and Selected Last Poems* was published by Ronsdale Press in 2005.

John Goodby lectures in English at Swansea University and co-organises the annual Hay Poetry Jamboree. His most recent poetry publications are *Illennium* (Shearsman, 2010) and *A True Prize* (Cinnamon, 2011); his latest critical book is *Work of Words: Re-reading the Poetry of Dylan Thomas* (Liverpool University Press, forthcoming 2013). He is currently working on a new edition of Thomas's collected poems for publication in the poet's centenary year, 2014.

Rob Inglis, artistic director of Musical Flying Squad, dramatizes local history, and with ArtsXchange @ King'sX, formed after 7/7, shares culture. His English versions of Botan's poems are agreed in discussion. Rob also works with the Bengali community. After journalism in Australia he acted with London companies and toured with solo shows.

Maria Jastrzębska's most recent collection is *Everyday Angels* from Waterloo Press (2009). She co-translated *Elsewhere* – selected poems by Iztok Osojnik, with Ana Jelnikar (Pighog Press, 2011). A co-editor of several anthologies, she won the Off Press International Writing Competition 2009. Her drama *Dementia Diaries* has been touring nationally. www.south-pole.org.uk

Originally from Colorado, **Timothy Kercher** now lives in Kyiv, Ukraine after living in the Republic of Georgia for four years, where he has been translating contemporary Georgian poetry. His poems and translations have appeared or are forthcoming in a number of recent literary publications, among them *Crazyhorse*, *Plume* and *Versal*.

Janet Kofi-Tsekpo studied English Language & Literature at the University of Manchester, and a multidisciplinary MA at the School of Oriental & African Studies (SOAS), University of London. Her writing has appeared in *Wasafiri, les cahiers de la femme, PN Review, Poetry Review, Ten, New Poetries V* and elsewhere.

Ilmar Lehtpere has translated seven books by Kristiina Ehin, including Popescu Prize winner *The Drums of Silence* (Oleander 2007), PBS Recommended Translation *The Scent of Your Shadow* (Arc 2010) and, most recently, *The Final Going of Snow* (*MPT* Poets 2011). More Kristiina Ehin translations are in preparation.

Ieva Lešinska-Gaber, born 1958 in Riga, worked and studied in the USA, moved to Sweden in 1987, and now lives in Riga, working as a free-lance journalist and translator. She has translated various English and American poets into Latvian, and has published English translations of poems and prose by Latvian authors in periodicals and anthologies in the UK and the US, including *Six Latvian Poets* (Arc Publications, 2011).

Michael Mackmin is editor of *The Rialto* poetry magazine. His own poems appear in other magazines and recently in two pamphlets, *Twenty Three Poems* (2006) and *From There to Here* (2011), from Happen*Stance*. Born in Croydon, he lives in Norfolk.

Sigurður A. Magnússon was born in 1928. He is a writer and a translator. Sigurður has translated English, Danish, Greek and German authors, among them H.C. Andersen, Bertolt Brecht, Walt Whitman, James Joyce, Nagíb Mahfúz, Kazuo Ishiguro, John Fowles and Ernest Hemingway.

Sarah Maguire is the founder and director of the Poetry Translation Centre and the author of four highly-acclaimed collections of poetry, including *The Pomegranates of Kandahar* (2007).

Gonzalo Melchor was born and grew up in Spain, was educated in the US and currently lives in London. His translations have appeared or are forthcoming in *Poetry*, *Poetry London* and *Poetry Review*.

Joel Mitchell lived in Mauritania for two years, from 2004-2006, while working with an NGO focused on maternal-child health. His exposure to popular poetry in Mauritania and Sudan has inspired his current work on contemporary Arabic poetry, particularly in dialect. Joel is currently a PhD candidate at the University of London.

Ian Parks was one of the Poetry Society New Poets in 1996. His collections include *Shell Island* (2006), *Love Poems 1979-2009* and *The Landing Stage* (2010). He has been widely published in British and American magazines and newspapers. *The Exile's House* is published by Waterloo and *The Cavafy Variations* is due from Rack Press in 2013. He is the 2012 writer in residence at Gladstone's Library.

Angus Reid is a writer and filmmaker. He has published two volumes of poetry: *The Gift* and *White Medicine*; a third, *Book of Days*, is forthcoming. His films include *The Ring,* which won 'Best Central European Documentary Feature' at Jihlava IDDF, but which has yet to be screened in the UK.

John M. Ridland was the 2010 Balassi Memorial Sword laureate for translations of Hungarian poetry, including Sándor Petöfi's *John the Valiant.* He has published his own poems in over a dozen books, with the latest, *Happy in an Ordinary Thing,* to come out in 2013 from Truman State University Press.

Claudia Rosenzweig, a graduate in Classical Studies from the University of Milan, specializes in Yiddish Literature in Renaissance Italy. Co-author of *Yiddish in Italia* (Milan 2003) and author of *Elye Bokher, Due canti yiddish* (Arezzo 2010), she is completing her edition of *Bovo d'Antona*, a 16th-century Yiddish rewriting of an Italian work in *ottava rima.*

Anthony Rudolf's book of prose and verse sequences *Zigzag* was published by Carcanet/Northern House in 2010. His memoir *Silent Conversations: A Reader's Life* is coming from Seagull Books (distributed by Chicago University Press) in September 2012. A volume of short stories is ready for publication and he has completed new essays on Yves Bonnefoy and Primo Levi.

Anna Selby is the programmer for Poetry Parnassus and works as Literature and Spoken Word Co-ordinator at the Southbank Centre.

Lynn M. Selby, M.A. 2005, is a Ph.D. candidate in anthropology in the African Diaspora Program at the University of Texas at Austin. She conducts her research in New York and Haiti and is finishing her dissertation on Haitian women's community activism and participation in popular politics in Port-au-Prince, Haiti.

Cameron Hawke Smith learnt Latin at school but taught himself Greek and took an external degree at London University in the subject (when it was still possible to do this). He also holds an MA in Aegean Prehistory and a PhD in Archaeology. He is currently trying to learn Gaelic through translating the works of Sorley MacLean.

Saradha Soobrayen is a freelance poetry and reviews editor and works as mentor and coach providing professional development for emerging and established writers and artists. Her poetry appears in the *Red Anthology* 2009, *The Forward Anthology 2008*, and *Oxford Poets Anthology 2007*. She received an Eric Gregory Award in 2004.

Armine Tamrazian was born in Tehran of Armenian parents and was educated in Armenian, Farsi and English. She holds a Ph.D in Linguistics from University College London. She has worked as a lecturer and has published four volumes of literary translations.

Stephen Watts is a poet, translator & editor. His most recent book is *Journey Across Breath/Tragitto nel respiro* 2011 from Hearing Eye, & *The Language Of It* is due from Shearsman in 2012.

MPT Subscription Form

Name	Address
Phone	Postcode
E-mail	Country

I would like to subscribe to *Modern Poetry in Translation* (please tick relevant box):

Subscription Rates (including postage by surface mail)

	UK	Overseas
❑ One year subscription (2 issues)	£19.90	£25 / US$ 42
❑ Two year subscription (4 issues) with discount	£36	£46 / US$ 77

Student Discount*

❑ One year subscription (2 issues)	£16	£21 / US$ 35
❑ Two year subscription (4 issues)	£28	£38 / US$ 63

Please indicate which year you expect to complete your studies 20 . . .

Standing Order Discount (only available to UK subscribers)

❑ Annual subscription (2 issues)	£18
❑ Student rate for annual subscription (2 issues)*	£14

Payment Method (please tick appropriate box)

❑ **Cheque:** please make cheques payable to: *Modern Poetry in Translation.* Sterling, US Dollar and Euro cheques accepted.

❑ **Standing Order:** please complete the standing order request below, indicating the date you would like your first payment to be taken. This should be at least one month after you return this form. We will set this up directly with your bank. Subsequent annual payments will be taken on the same date each year. For UK only.

Bank Name	Account Name
Branch Address	❑ Please notify my bank
	Please take my first payment on
Post Code	......./......./......... and future payments on
Sort Code	the same date each year.
Account Number	Signature:
	Date........./........./............

Bank Use Only: In favour of Modern Poetry in Translation, Lloyds TSB, 1 High St, Carfax, Oxford, OX1 4AA, UK a/c 03115155 Sort-code 30-96-35

Please return this form to: The Administrator, Modern Poetry in Translation, The Queen's College, Oxford, OX1 4AW   administrator@mptmagazine/www.mptmagazine.com